Acclaim for
Brujas, bultos, y brasas:
Tales of Witchcraft and the Supernatural in the Pecos Valley
and for Nasario García

Nasario García ha conseguido en esta última obra una espléndida y rara combinación entre la calidad literaria y el rigor social y antropológico. Para un español con interés en las raíces hispánicas del Sudoeste de los Estados Unidos, *Brujas, bultos, y brasas* constituye una lectura fascinante, por haber recuperado antiguas leyendas y anécdotas de aquellas eras, que sitúan esta recopilación al nivel del clásico de Juan B. Rael: *Cuentos españoles de Colorado y Nuevo México.*

—Eduardo Garrigues, Embajador Español, Namibia, Autor,
The Grass Rains

Nasario García has managed to blend in this last work a splendid and unique combination of literary quality along with a certain social and anthropological precision. For a Spaniard with an interest in Hispanic roots in the southwestern United States, *Brujas, bultos, y brasas* constitutes fascinating reading which places this compilation of legends and anecdotes from yesteryear at the level of Juan B. Rael's classic work, *Cuentos españoles de Colorado y Nuevo México.*

—Eduardo Garrigues, Spanish Ambassador, Namibia, Author,
The Grass Rains

Brujas, bultos, y brasas is a most delightful and enticing *chef-d'oeuvre* in which Nasario García records incidents of witchcraft, of neighbors under a spell, of sightings of mysterious sparks, and inexplicable lights among Hispanics who lead an idyllic pastoral life in a never-never land that we have come to call the Land of Enchantment.

—Rubén Cobos, Author,
Dictionary of New Mexico and Southern Colorado Spanish

Acts of genius are the simplest things. Nasario García is the genius and this book is his act. Collecting the stories and traditions of people, then presenting them in a bilingual format is the very substance, the basis, of all good history.

—Tom E. Chávez, Director, *Palace of the Governors, Museum of New Mexico*

BRUJAS, BULTOS, Y BRASAS

TALES OF WITCHCRAFT
and the
SUPERNATURAL
in the Pecos Valley

Collected and Edited by Nasario García

Foreword by Marc Simmons
Principal Photography by Nedra Westwater

Western
Edge Press

DEDICATORIA
to RUBÉN COBOS
and SABINE R. ULIBARRÍ

Two wonderful friends and indefatigable champions of
Hispanic culture of New Mexico

Photography Credits:

Frontispiece: Petrita Sandoval, circa 1930, maternal grandmother
of Pedro V. Gallegos. Courtesy Pedro V. Gallegos
Photos by Geri Salazar: Pages 28, 60, 80, 104, 112, 118, 182
Photos by author: Pages 2, 84, 140
Photo by Jan M. Smith-García: Page 32

Map on page 2 by Deborah Reade

Second printing, 2001

ISBN: 1-889921-03-3

LC: 99-071006

FIRST EDITION

Western Edge Press
126 Candelario Street
Santa Fe, New Mexico 87501
505.988.7214   •   westernedge@santa-fe.net

Design by Jim Mafchir
Edited by Nancy Zimmerman

ACKNOWLEDGMENTS

Completing a book is somewhat analogous to a puzzle—the whole comprises many distinct parts. From cover to cover, the spirit that vibrates throughout each and every page is a reflection not only of the author's personal work and interest, but of the countless people who have contributed in a significant and unselfish way toward seeing the publication become a reality. Their invaluable contributions, both large and small, are hereby acknowledged in *Brujas, bultos, y brasas: Tales of Witchcraft and the Supernatural in the Pecos Valley.*

Above all, I want to express my sincere appreciation to all the people of the Pecos Valley who have given generously of their time and of themselves over the years. Allowing me time and again to walk into their homes to pry into their past is something I shall always treasure. Those whose narratives appear in my book are acknowledged for their contribution, while others whose stories are absent have a special place in my heart, and hopefully their stories will form part of a future publication.

There are other special people whom I would like to single out for their generous assistance as well. No trip to the Pecos Valley was ever complete without visiting and consulting with Don Pedro V. Gallegos and his wife, Josephine, both lifelong residents of Villanueva. He is the consummate *caballero* (gentleman), and she a grand lady, both of whom never hesitated to offer me information or to supply names of people to contact in order to broaden my knowledge of El Valle. A note of singular thanks goes to three of my former students, Rosabel Gallegos, Félix Vigil, and George Gallegos, whose participation contributed immeasurably to my project. I also want to thank Geri Salazar and Isabel López for their part in this endeavor.

Special thanks are due two personal friends of mine, Nedra Westwater for her excellent photographs, and Tom Chávez, director of the Palace of the Governors, for his critical reading of portions of my manuscript.

No publication can be brought to a successful conclusion without some kind of financial assistance from time to time. Individuals who see merit in your work often take the bold risk of helping you through funding in order to see your work completed. I want to thank Tobías Luján, director of the Center for Regional Studies at the University of New Mexico, the New Mexico Endowment for the Humanities, and the Office of Research and Sponsored Projects at New Mexico Highlands University for research grants awarded me to conduct some of my field work.

Last but certainly not least, a debt of sincere gratitude is due Nancy Zimmerman, an ally throughout the editing process. Her illuminating suggestions and ideas underscore the fundamental importance of a good copy editor.

Contents

San Miguel Fiestas

Foreword

*T*here exist many approaches to the study of New Mexico's Hispanic culture, each with its own individual merit and appeal. I am especially partial, however, to the method employed by author and scholar Nasario García, who conducts his research literally from the ground up. It has become his practice, as demonstrated in a series of earlier books on the Río Puerco valley, to interview *los viejitos*, old-timers, recording and publishing their recollections in the original Spanish, together with an English translation.

The resulting narratives, I find, catch the spirit and essence of the old way of life about as well as it can now be done. Without García's dedicated tale-collecting over many years, a vast storehouse of cultural material would have slipped away, impossible for future generations to recover.

In the present work, *Brujas, bultos, y brasas: Tales of Witchcraft and the Supernatural in the Pecos Valley*, García shifts his focus from the Río Puerco to the valley of the Pecos—or at least a 15-mile stretch of it between the villages of San José and Villanueva, an area containing some of the oldest settlements on the eastern side of New Mexico. It turns out, for his purposes, to be as productive a field as the one he left behind.

This circumscribed section of the Pecos basin emerged in the early nineteenth century as a separate *patria chica*, a largely self-contained and insular little homeland, for which the residents developed strong feelings of loyalty and affection. Indeed, numbers of them scarcely ever ventured outside, into the world beyond. In former times, there may even have been small cultural distinctions, such as habits of speech or daily customs, that set these people slightly apart from other New Mexicans.

As García demonstrates, however, the insularity has broken down in the twentieth century, with out-migration and a serious decline in population. Of those people who remain, quite a few commute daily to jobs in Las Vegas, or even Santa Fe, significantly diminishing the sense of isolation. Still, the attachment to El Valle and the finding of one's sense of identity there, on that special piece of natal earth, has not been entirely lost.

From the deep well of Pecos Valley folklore, García in this book draws mainly upon the realm of the supernatural. The world of demons and malevolent magic has long exercised a hold over the imagination of Southwestern peoples. In the stories and vignettes included here, readers can gain insights into the rich inner life of El Valle dwellers, a life that intermingles deep fear of otherwordly powers with a supreme faith in the protective efficacy of religious prescriptions and ceremonies. Sophisticated urbanites of today will probably be surprised to observe that from seemingly simple rural folk there comes such a bounty of imaginative and varied images that seem to have about them creative elements of true art.

In the early 1970s I, too, collected some oral history from this precinct of the Pecos Valley, although little if any of it was directly related to the supernatural. I was impressed then by the availability of innumerable possibilities for research. Nasario García in his *Brujas, bultos, y brasas* has competently mined one of those veins, giving us a vivid picture of Hispanic witchlore in its many dimensions. I am grateful that he has invited me to contribute a foreword to his book and pleased that I can recommend it to all those with a sincere interest in Hispanic folkways of the Southwest.

—*Marc Simmons*
Cerrillos, NM

BRUJAS, BULTOS, Y BRASAS

TALES OF WITCHCRAFT
and the
SUPERNATURAL
in the Pecos Valley

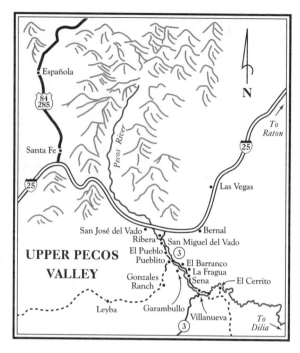

ABOVE: *Map of the villages of El Valle showing their proximity to roads and the Pecos River.*
BELOW: *The village of Villanueva.*

Introduction

INTRODUCTION

*I*n 1986, after being away from New Mexico for 22 years while teaching in Pennsylvania, Illinois, and Colorado, I finally returned to my home state. Las Vegas, New Mexico, while somewhat removed from my native Río Puerco valley northwest of Albuquerque, provided me an opportunity, nonetheless, to set anchor in a region where I could justifiably claim roots to my past on both sides of my family. For one thing, my maternal great-grandmother was born in Mora, north of Las Vegas, while my paternal grandmother, whom I grew up with on the Río Puerco ranch, was born in Pecos. These links to the region made me feel at ease in Las Vegas and its outlying communities, including those in the Río Pecos valley.

In 1989 I was fortunate to have a student from the Río Pecos valley in one of my classes. She spoke proudly of the region, her community, and its citizens. As I probed about the *viejitos* (old-timers), their language, customs, and traditions, I became more and more intrigued with what I heard. I set about conducting a series of oral interviews with the local residents, and with each trip to the Río Pecos valley, I was increasingly fascinated by the vibrant lode of Hispanic culture waiting to be mined from the old folks.

Over time, *Brujas, bultos, y brasas: Tales of Witchcraft and the Supernatural in the Pecos Valley*, a compilation of magic and folklore from the valley known to the locals as El Valle (Map 1), was born. El Valle is minuscule in terms of the overall course of the Pecos River (the Río Pecos flows 900 miles from the headwaters in the Sangre de Cristo Mountains east of Santa Fe and joins the Río Grande before emptying into the Gulf of Mexico), but of vital importance to those of us interested in the past. Somewhat self-contained, it stretches from San José, about 25 miles southwest of Las Vegas, to Villanueva, a distance of about 15 winding miles. In between are Ribera, El Pueblo, Sena (El Puertecito), and San Miguel. The founding of these agricultural settlements came about as a result of San Miguel's influence as a commerce center during the heyday of the Santa Fe Trail. Aside from these communities with a well-established history, there are hamlets that do not even dot the New Mexico map (e.g., El Barranco, Lobato, Sacatosa, El Ranchito), where some of my interviewees reside.

Now I invite you to accompany me into the Río Pecos valley to become acquainted with the villages of these proud people. Upon entering the valley, a kind of a serenity seems to put one at ease regardless of the time of year. The mesas to the north and south of the meandering Pecos River appear to watch over El Valle and its people like protective parents, and the valley itself opens and closes like a treasure chest with each changing season. Whether it be a snowy winter, a blustery spring, a sultry summer, or a cloud-filled fall, each season is a sonata unto itself.

In late March or early April one can witness the raw vitality of a group of men—young and old—cleaning the ditches along with the *mayordomo* (ditch boss) in preparation for releasing the spring waters from the Pecos River for irrigation. The plowing of the fertile red soil for planting corn has become a weekend activity, since most landowners have regular jobs during the week. On some properties one sees the alfalfa or hay beginning to sprout. Older folks till the soil of their home gardens, getting them ready to plant *calabacitas* (squash), *pepinos* (cucumbers), melons, tomatoes, corn, and, of course, the ubiquitous chile. Still others begin to examine the apple, peach, plum, or apricot trees in their orchards or front yards for any pruning deemed necessary.

Signs of life are seen in other ways. Spring and summer are when women hang their clothes outdoors on *perchas* (clotheslines) to dry the old-fashioned way, even though many of them own automatic dryers. Here and there you will spot an elderly man fixing fence posts, casualties of a cold, bitter winter, as well as a boy chopping wood (chain saws are more popular) for his grandparents' *fogón* (pot-bellied stove) or *estufa* (kitchen stove), both still permanent fixtures in many of the old-timers' households. Even dogs seem to come out from hibernation to bark at passing cars, as though they know that you are not a valley resident.

Sluice gate of acequia *(irrigation ditch) leading from the Pecos River.*

On occasion I have visited people in El Valle in August and September, the time of year when people reap the fruits of their labor—from cutting hay, harvesting corn, and picking vegetables from their gardens to drying chile or canning fruit for the winter months. Some people own dairy cows, goats, or sheep, so it is not unusual to walk into their homes and be offered *requesón* (home-made cheese) with jelly or syrup and a cup of coffee, spiced with a story or two from yesteryear.

We begin our journey in picturesque San José, founded in 1803. It is a huddle of stone houses, earth-toned adobe dwellings, and mobile homes perched on a hilltop surrounded by colorful mesas and the piñon- and juniper-clad foothills of the snow-capped Sangre de Cristo Mountains to the north. San José sits like an acropolis adjacent to the Pecos River, its pastoral setting embracing visitors. The homes surrounding the plaza and the church, like a *colcha* (bedspread) protecting its child, welcome you into a corridor of beauty and elegance.

From San José the valley extends south to the village of

Introduction

Villanueva atop another foothill. The expanse in between these villages forms a pastoral tableau of bucolic simplicity and beauty: cows and horses lounging in their paddocks; farmers tending unhurriedly to their tasks; magpies calling to one another from the cottonwood trees and bushes that line the Pecos River, the gushing waters that give life to this magical valley. Those turbulent years when the Spanish settlers battled marauding bands of Comanches and Jicarilla Apaches seem distant indeed.

And yet it was as recently as 1821, when the Santa Fe Trail began its reign as the dominant trade route of the region, that the valley rose to prominence as a commercial and agricultural center. San Miguel, founded in 1794 on a grant approved by Governor Fernando Chacón and one of the first and most important colonizations in the Upper Pecos valley (Map 2), became an important cog in the wheel of Hispanic expansion and economic trade east of the Río Grande valley. After Mexico's independence from Spain in 1821, it opened up an international trade that benefitted both Mexicans and Americans while expanding San Miguel's economy, as thousands of dollars' worth of merchandise was transported across the lonely, unforgiving prairies from the States.

The principal villages—San José, Ribera, San Miguel, El Pueblo, Sena, and Villanueva—all boast their own personalities. And while the physical layout varies from one community to another, they all share common features, such as a central church and cemetery, that bind them together like chiles on a *ristra*. The diversity in architecture is another similarity; it is not unusual to find a historic adobe home or stone edifice existing alongside a mobile home. Prefabricated structures and newly built homes with modern architectural designs add to the overall contrast of old versus new that characterizes the villages of El Valle.

Within this mosaic of contrasts and similarities, some communities stand out because of their simplicity; others command our attention because of their charm. Ribera, for example, a small unobtrusive place, extends to the hillsides east of the main road and is split by the railroad tracks that run east and west. Except for a new post office, which serves the local community, San Miguel, and other hamlets, Ribera consists entirely of a mere smattering of homes. There are no commercial outlets, although at least one family has

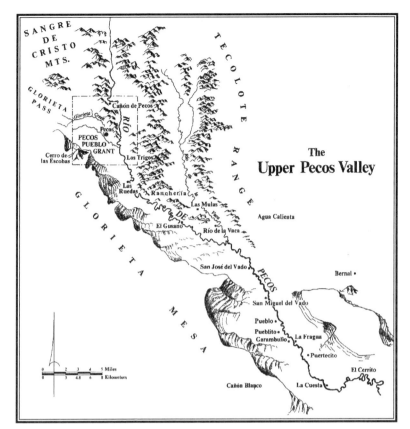

Map of the Upper Pecos Valley from Kiva, Cross, and Crown: The Pecos Indians and New Mexico 1540–1840, *John Kessell; published by the National Park Service, U.S. Department of the Interior, 1979; reprinted by the University of New Mexico Press, 1987.*

begun to grow and sell organic garlic.

Every time I visit El Valle I am reminded that while some things do change, others remain the same. The magnificent San Miguel church with its twin towers, finished between 1806 and 1811, appears essentially the same today as when Lieutenant James Williams Abert sketched it in 1846 during his trip along the Santa Fe Trail. Yet, a mere 100 yards away at the southern edge of San Miguel, there stands a beautiful new building, San Miguel del Vado Senior Citizens Center, which opened its doors in April of 1997.

As we leave San Miguel and head south amid rolling hills along

San Miguel Church.

a winding road, we suddenly come upon El Pueblo, with its ceme-tery on a hillside and its church, San Antonio, smack in the middle of the community. The homes around the church appear to act as a protective shield, while the church's proximity to people's dwellings seems to remind them that spiritual guidance and solace are but a few feet from their doorsteps.

About a quarter of a mile to the south is an extension of El Pueblo, a kind of miniature "suburb." This area features a few homes, a combined bar/gasoline station, and a body shop across the street. One or two old adobe homes lie in a state of disrepair. As we leave El Pueblo and proceed east across the Pecos River, following the contours of the river and the *acequia* (irrigation ditch), small settlements such as El Barranco and La Fragua come into our path. Upon approaching Sena, a few new mobile and prefabricated homes pepper the landscape along with old abandoned adobe dwellings, reminders of families who once inhabited El Valle but who now find themselves far away from their native land.

Sena bears the name of the famous seventeenth-century

Bernardo de Sena, better known for the Sena Plaza in Santa Fe. Today it is a small, quiet community with descendants of the Sena clan still counted among its inhabitants. Sena closed its post office not long ago, but it still has a beautiful, well-kept church, plus a small grocery store whose owners operate it from their home.

Leaving Sena behind, our winding journey along the Pecos River continues as the *acequia* mimics its course. Suddenly, after passing through El Vallito de Piedra and rounding a mesa, there looms Villanueva, once known as La Cuesta. It was founded between 1805 and 1818, notwithstanding the fact that it began as a walled *placita* (village) settlement during the late 1700s, according to Beverly Spears (*Amerian Adobes: Rural House of Northern New Mexico,* UNM Press, 1986). Villanueva's founders were José Felipe Madrid and Mariano Baros, both of whom still have descendants living in El Valle.

Of all the villages here, Villanueva is perhaps the most active and dynamic. Much of this energy surrounds the local church, Nuestra Señora de Guadalupe. Groundbreaking for the church evidently took place in 1826, perhaps even as early as 1818, but it was not completed and sanctified until about 1830.

9

For more than 150 years, Villanueva parishioners have played a vital role in maintaining religious traditions such as the patron saint's day, mass, baptisms, weddings, rosaries, and novenas. An important and proud feature of the church is the 265-foot embroidered tapestry woven in 1976 by 36 local women as part of the Bicentennial celebration. This embroidery reflects an unequivocal and united spirituality within the community that prevails to the present time.

Perhaps the endeavor most venerated throughout the years by the inhabitants of Villanueva is the Grotto of Our Lady of Guadalupe, commonly referred to as La Gruta. Completed in 1956, it overlooks the village from a hill just north of town, and every August 15 since 1956, local residents have paid homage to the Virgin by conducting a pilgrimage to the Grotto. Today the Grotto is the pride of every young and old Villanuevan who still adheres to certain personal, cultural, and religious beliefs and principles. As Villanueva resident Don Pedro V. Gallegos, the main caretaker of La Gruta, said to me not long ago: "I think that if you really believe in a thing as holy as this [the Grotto], and you go up there to pray and put yourself in God's hands, you set your mind at ease and feel good inside. When you come down, you can sleep. Your heart and soul are satisfied and closer to God."

Countless times I have packed my lunch and visited the Grotto, and each time I was amazed to discover that even on a blustery day, the serenity of El Valle not only seems to begin and intensify with the Grotto, but to culminate with it as well. As I glance across time and space from the Grotto—as I have done many times—the history and splendor of this valley and the wonderful people who live there inevitably occupy my thoughts. Words like honesty, decency, and humility come to mind as best describing these people. It is not difficult to explain why I feel comfortable in their homeland, as though I were a longstanding *vecino* (neighbor) of theirs. After all, their environment is very similar to what mine was like in the Río Puerco valley. At present, however, El Valle's facade and spirit have begun to change.

Actually, the character of El Valle began to change as far back as 1835 with the founding of Las Vegas, New Mexico, as this town took over much of San Miguel's important trade along the Santa Fe Trail. The population of the Río Pecos valley began to decline shortly thereafter. The arrival of the railroad in 1879, which passed through Las Vegas en route to Albuquerque, further exacerbated the population loss.

Throughout the next 50 years, the population of the Río Pecos valley continued to dwindle. The Great Depression of the 1930s, coupled with World War II, made matters even worse for El Valle. Many men left the valley in search of jobs with the railroad elsewhere in New Mexico and Colorado, as well as in coal mines, steel mills, or government programs. What's more, young men discharged from military service after World War II declined to return to El Valle for lack of employment opportunities, so the population continued to plummet throughout the 1940s and '50s.

This phenomenon, while having slowed down, continues to date. Nevertheless, during the past two to three years a few people have begun to return to their native villages following retirement, thus adding modestly to the population. But the prospects for significant population growth are gloomy at best.

Not long ago, when I would drive through the Río Pecos valley, I would find few signs, if any, advertising land or properties for sale. At most an unassuming sign reading "For Sale by Owner" could be spotted. Today, however, more sophisticated and high-profile signs by real-estate companies acting as agents for landowners are popping up throughout El Valle.

Not only have the times changed in just a few years, but people's attitudes as well. Some of the old-timers no longer believe they should hold on to their property for their children and grandchildren to inherit. Rather, they want to able to enjoy the monies from the land sales while they are still alive. Their decision to sell stems in many cases from their own children's lack of interest in the land.

The implications of this attitude are twofold: It means a depletion of landholdings that have been in families for generations and, in most cases, the new property owners will not be Hispanic or natives of El Valle (both phenomena have already begun to occur), thus changing its demographics. In recent times San José and its sister communities have become home to artists disenchanted with other so-called art colonies. Newcomers to the valley simply wish to live in a rural setting away from the urban trappings of larger communities and cities.

On the surface, one would think that these recent arrivals would bolster the diminishing population but, in fact, their numbers are modest at best and hardly offset the passing away of the old-timers. So, it is fair to say that at the present time senior citizens are "winning" the race, but once they pass on, their voices will be silenced forever unless a more concerted effort is made to rescue their oral histories while they are still living.

Most people have yet to realize the importance of oral tradition in our day and age of technological frenzy, a time when Hispanos in particular should be striving in earnest to rescue as much of our heritage from oblivion as possible so that our children and grandchildren can enjoy it. The manner in which old-timers' oral stories can affect you, as they have affected me not only personally and culturally, but professionally, is inexpressible. At the same time, my contribution to the study of oral history and folklore during the past 20 years seems minimal in comparison with the wealth of information the old folks have to offer. But their sea of knowledge and wisdom is rapidly shrinking as they depart this earth. Soon, when there is nothing more to record, we will be left to regret the efforts not undertaken in time.

Pride and positive attitudes in El Valle among influential Hispanos have served to keep their language, customs, and traditions from fading or disappearing altogether. The local church remains the center of camaraderie and personal spirituality, serving as the heart and soul of every Hispano community in the Pecos Valley—as elsewhere in Northern New Mexico— and bringing people together, above all during their yearly *función* (religious ceremony). This esprit de corps continues strong to this day among many residents of El Valle. Their relative isolation, despite the demands on people's time and our rapidly changing society, has enabled the Río Pecoans to preserve their language and culture as a unique window on the past.

The challenge is a formidable one indeed because, as the elders pass away, very few young men and women are waiting to assume their roles. This problem, made patently clear in 1989 when I first began to interview the people of this lovely region, was repeated more recently when a disconsolate Don Pedro Gallegos said to me: *"Ya la plebe de hoy en día no tiene interés. Ya no les importa. No sé qué va pasar cuando nosotros [los viejos] ya no estemos aquí. Yo creo que se va perder todo lo que hemos cuidao."* ("Today's youth aren't interested. They don't care anymore. I don't know what's going to happen when we [the old folks] are no longer around. I believe everything we've preserved is going to be lost.")

Don Pedro Gallegos's words ring both of nostalgia and realism. To envision his beloved valley without many of the cultural practices that he and his fellow citizens have promoted over the years, such as the oral storytelling tradition that has been a mainstay in the local communities up and down the Río Pecos valley, is to lose something very precious and close to his heart.

One would venture to say that there is no Hispano, including this author, who grew up in rural New Mexico within the last 40 or 50 years who is not capable of recounting an eerie story or two related to witchcraft and its supernatural trappings, thanks to the prominent role of la *agüelita* (grandmother). We as grandchildren at the

San José Church.

ranch looked up to my paternal grandmother as the principal story-teller responsible for entertaining (or frightening) us at bedtime. Given her versatility as a raconteur, her narratives ranged from pleasant fairy-tale-type stories to those that scared the dickens out of us, such as *la cosa mala* (an evil spirit) or *el coco* (the bogeyman).

As a small boy I heard scores of stories of the supernatural that are recounted in one form or another up and down the Río Pecos valley. Recollections of *brujas* (witches), *el diablo* (the devil), *bultos* (ghosts), *el mal ojo* (the evil eye), *una persona enyerbada* (a bewitched person), and many other superstitions are but a few examples. We siblings invariably were even beneficiaries (or victims!) of a trick or two coming from our own parents playing the role of bogeyman.

Some animals in El Valle that purportedly possessed supernatural powers (often identical to the ones that I grew up with) were *el burrito* (the donkey), snakes, the coyote, and *el tecolote* or *la lechuza* (the owl).

There were other superstitious beliefs prevalent in my household, also mentioned by residents of the Río Pecos valley, that dealt with sorcery-like powers. For example, if my brother or I went to milk a cow in the morning and found that it had no milk, it was believed that a *mamona* (a milk snake) had sucked the milk from the cow's udder; thereafter, the cow's udder went dry, we were told, due to the snake's evil intrusion.

Teenage daughters or granddaughters were admonished by their mothers or grandmothers never to swim nude in *charcos grandes de agua* (large pools of waters) that had formed after a rainstorm or flood along the riverbed where *guajolotes* or *tepocates* (tadpoles) hibernated. The hazard of these little amphibians penetrating the girls' bodies and getting them pregnant was dramatized as fact and not fiction (we boys shrugged off the notion as merely a ploy to keep the girls away from us). This subject is not alien to residents of El Valle.

Perhaps no single type of story fascinated me more than those concerning the supernatural. Whether related to balls of fire, *polvitos* (witch powders), sparks emitting from a chimney in an old abandoned adobe home, a *farol* (lantern) burning brightly at night in my grandfather's empty house while he was away, chains rattling at night, or finding shiny apples on our doorstep, all contained magical power or an evil element of sorts (*la cosa mala*) that intrigued me.

Children of past generations have been fascinated by stories related to the supernatural. As the eminent historian Marc Simmons reminds us in his excellent work, *Witchcraft in the Southwest: Spanish and Indian Supernaturalism on the Río Grande* (Northland Press, 1974), "Practically every adobe hamlet and town on the Río Grande [especially New Mexico] once possessed its own stories and traditions of witches, were-animals, and supernatural events."

Since the late 1980s, I have made countless trips to El Valle to interview and to photograph dozens of residents on a variety of subjects related to their lives in their villages. On each occasion, whether I was meeting someone for the first time or renewing old acquaintances, I was greeted with open arms. In every instance I was enriched by their reminiscences and words of wisdom.

At the time of the interviews (1989–1996) the 26 men and

women featured in *Brujas, bultos, y brasas: Tales of Witchcraft and the Supernatural in the Pecos Valley* were in their 60s, 70s, 80s, and 90s. One of the most endearing qualities about the people from El Valle is their positive outlook on life. As they reflect on their lives, they do so with a great sense of contentment. Now in their golden years, they are very much at peace with themselves, for they sense in their own hearts that their mission as parents, grandparents, and community people, through good and bad times, has been fulfilled and hence brought them a special happiness for which they are thankful.

The storytellers in this corpus of oral literature, each with a distinct personality, are proud and humble people who expressed a special enthusiasm as they related the stories on witchcraft in their own manner and style. At times the interviewees invoked their own humor, as we see in Pablo Aguilar from Sena, who pokes fun at a rival village in "*¡Son las brujas de Villanueva!*" ("They're the Witches from Villanueva!"). Other times the narratives are more serious in tone, especially if the narrator plays a central role. Good examples are Lala Gallegos's story, "*A mí han hecho tantos males*" ("I've Been Bewitched so Many Times"), in which death comes knocking at her door on more than one occasion, or Valerio García's "*Vi como bultos*" ("I Saw What Looked like Ghosts), where illusions become reality. Viviana Tapia's own account titled, "*Me habían hecho mal en el durazno*" ("Someone Had Bewitched My Peaches") dramatizes the dire consequences of unknowingly eating enchanted fruit. Then there is Nobertita Tafoya y Padilla's tragic episode of her sister who lost her eyesight due to the evil eye. "*Perdió los ojos*" ("She Lost her Eyesight") is a gripping account one will not easily forget.

15

Other stories, perhaps not as dramatic as this last one, contain moral underpinnings aimed at sons and daughters or the population as a whole. Endalecio P. Sena's "*El dinero hace ruido*" ("Money Makes Noise") reminds us that the love of money is not only the root of all evil, but it affects all of us, whereas Carmel Ulibarrí in her story, "*Te va llevar el diablo*" ("The Devil's Going to Take You Away"), aimed at children, clearly suggests its own moral admonition if they misbehave. But unscrupulous behavior of a different kind, at a distinct level, applied more to grownups. This is made patently clear in "*Era de estos mujereros*" ("He Was One of These Womanizers"), by Rosavé M. Lucero, about an indiscreet newlywed who changed his ways and became contrite after an encounter with diabolic creatures.

Regardless of the nature of the stories, their central themes, their narrators, or what village they come from, the mother tongue and everyday mode of communication is Spanish. Their linguistic world has been, and continues to be, one-dimensional in scope but an invaluable asset to us all.

Language, we are reminded, is a powerful tool because it links people intimately with their culture. Both are mutually inclusive and inseparable; this partnership reflects their own personal beliefs, humor, delusions, inspirations, attitudes, discretions, and aberrations. Whatever cultural attribute is advanced, irrespective of the context in which it is articulated, the language of the culture is pivotal with each given sound, word, phrase, folk saying, or idiomatic expression.

The language employed by the old-timers in *Brujas, bultos, y brasas: Tales of Witchcraft and the Supernatural in the Pecos Valley* epitomizes this linguistic spirit. Contrary to popular belief in certain corners of New Mexico, the everyday lexicon is composed of standard Spanish (not the Castillian pronunciation of c+e or i = th), which can be understood by virtually everyone throughout the Spanish-speaking world (e.g., Spain and Latin America). True, this everyday Spanish is complemented by a smattering of regionalisms (*jallar/hallar, fiero/feo*), archaisms (*vido/vio, hicites/hiciste*), and Anglicisms (*daime/dime*), and (*bonche/bunch*), but these linguistic nuances merely enhance the richness of the language. Idiomatic expressions indigenous to local communities in El Valle are not uncommon.

A varied pronunciation of the same word among Spanish-speakers in Northern New Mexico, often contained in a single story or paragraph (e.g., *pues/pos/pus*), is not considered unorthodox or peculiar among inhabitants of the Río Pecos valley. In the main, speech patterns and circumflex idiosyncrasies reflect both environment and the people's raison d'être.

Their narrative styles, each distinct, are remarkably clear and cohesive. Some editing, however, was necessary. Minor revisions were made in cases where repetition of pause words or expressions occurred to eliminate monotony, cacophony, incoherences, or non

_16_

sequiturs within the internal structure of the stories. Changes in syntax were sometimes essential to improve the narrative quality of the stories. Making them as readable as possible was of paramount importance.

In transcribing the narratives, a conscious attempt was also made to maintain the integrity of the spoken language without putting it into so-called modern or standard Spanish. The voices that speak here are authentic, and they reflect a unique realism inherent in the stories themselves.

The recollections are arranged alphabetically by author, but progression from one story to another was taken into consideration for a smoother transition. Each story, preceded by biographical data and a photograph of the storyteller, is presented in Spanish and English. The same effort to uphold the integrity of the Spanish was invoked in the English translation. Conveying the thoughts behind people's words and expressions took precedence over verbatim translations that would otherwise yield tedious, trite, or unrealistic text. The ultimate objective was to sustain the life and spirit of the stories without sacrificing content and form.

A glossary juxtaposing regional Spanish terms with modern or standard usage as well as a list of defined witchcraft words and expressions and childhood superstitions appear at the end of the book. Many of these regional words or phrases are known to students of New Mexican Spanish. Others are less familiar, which reinforces the fact that language is inextricably bound to culture, and culture to language.

The stories, as mentioned at the outset, concern witches, buried treasures, the devil, the evil eye, the bogeyman, natural phenomena, even necromancy. These old-timers' recollections honor a world of enchantment defended passionately by some narrators. Others are a trifle cynical about their veracity, but even they enjoyed reminiscing. These tales constitute an integral part of the Hispano's cultural legacy to us and to our descendants. They no doubt will entertain and tickle the funny bone of some, but raise an eyebrow in others.

San Miguel Fiestas—Religious Procession

NARRATORS / NARRADORES

Pablo Aguilar

PABLO AGUILAR

Nació: El 3 de octubre, 1913
El Armario, NM
Entrevista: El 29 de agosto, 1989
Sena, NM

Born: October 3, 1913
El Armario, NM
Interview: August 29, 1989
Sena, NM

Espíritus malos

En una ocasión es que había este hombre que le llamaban muy bandolero, que le gustaba andar parriba y pabajo, en todos los bailes y funciones como loo se observan. De acuerdo con esto, los viejitos siempre le aconsejaban de que no anduviera tanto, que no juera tan anducio, que algo le podía pasar.

Mientras tanto, en una ocasión, se jue a un baile. En cuanto que iba al baile, ahi en el camino onde iba, oyó que estaba llorando un niño, y cuando él se dio cuenta, cayó en curia, y se jue pa onde estaba el niño. Y jue y agarró el niño y se lo echó [en brazos]—en esos entonces hacían sus viajes a caballo. Mientras tanto isque iba ahi en el camino, lo agarró al niño en brazos y se jue al baile, siempre. A poco que caminó el hombre—iba mal intencionao [el niño] seguro, ¿ves?—el cuento es que a poco que habló isque dijo:

—Mira papacito. Ya tengo dientes—. Y cuando vido eso, vido que salió llama de la boca del niño. Y lo tiró y se golvió [a casa].

Cuando cayó a la casa, pos, entró y nomás cayó y se desmayó. Pues hasta otro día en la mañana cuando se levantó, les contó la historia a los viejitos qué era lo que le había pasao. Se figuraba que se trataba de que podía ser un espíritu malo.

De modo que en otra ocasión también, había otro hombre del mismo tipo. Y éste también viajaba; le gustaba andar de bandolero paí y pacá. Mientras tanto iba en el camino onde iba. Ahi en la noche iba al baile o iba a sus tragedias.

Cuando iba él vido que iba una mota de lana adelante, brinco y brinco, brinco y brinco. Mientras tanto le pegó él al caballo un azote y brincó y le dio el hombre con la cuarta a la lana. Y cuando menos pensó, brincó la lana, una mota de lana a onde iba él. Se le subió en las ancas del caballo y lo agarró y lo abrazó. Era un espíritu malo.

Mientras tanto no jue al baile. Lo que resultó, asina como pudo, cuando resucitó, pus también se desmayó, cuando resucitó vino a la casa. Otro día les platicó el caso a sus padres, qué era lo que le había pasao. De ahi pa delante, se resumió en ya no volvió a pensar ni hacer nada más sus picardías como acostumbraba. Ése es lo que me platicaban mis agüelitos.

Pablo Aguilar

Evil Spirits

They say that once upon a time there was this man whom everybody thought of as being a real gadabout because he liked to go here and there, to all of the dances and functions that are usually celebrated. Accordingly, the little old men always advised him not to roam so much, for him not to be such a wanderer, because something could happen to him.

Nevertheless, on a certain occasion, he went to a dance. As he was headed for the dance, there on the road where he was traveling he heard a child crying, and when he noticed that, he became curious and headed to where the child was. He went and grabbed the child and took him into his arms—back then they traveled on horseback—and headed on to the dance anyway. No sooner had the man traveled a ways—the child had bad intentions, you see, so goes the story—when the child supposedly said to him, "Look daddy. I have teeth." And when the man looked, fire was coming out of the child's mouth. He tossed him down and rushed home.

When he got home, he went in and simply fell down in a faint. The next morning when he got up he told the little old men what had happened. The feeling was that it must have been an evil spirit.

It so happens that on another occasion, there was the same type of man. And this man also did a lot of traveling; he enjoyed being a gadabout, going here and there. So there he was on the road as usual. It was at night as he headed for the dance—or to flirt with misfortune.

On the road he saw a moving woolen ball ahead of him, jumping up and down, up and down. So he gave the horse a good whack and it jumped, and in doing so the man struck the woolen ball with his quirt. All of a sudden, when he least expected it, the woolen ball jumped up and climbed on the rump of the horse, that is, behind the rider, and it grabbed him and hugged him. It was an evil spirit.

And so he didn't go to the dance. What happened is this: As best he could manage, after he came to, because he too had fainted, when he came to, he went home. Next day he told his parents the whole thing, exactly what had happened. From then on, he resigned himself to never again go out and perform his usual chicanery. At least that's what my grandparents told me.

Pablo Aguilar

¡Son las brujas de Villanueva!

En otra ocasión, éste es caso que nos pasó—a mí y a mi mamá y a mi hermano. Y esto pasó aquí localmente ahi en Villanueva. Pues mi padrastro acostumbraba irse a trabajar como siempre, y mi mamá era de un distinto que pa ella no había ninguna cosa de tragedia. Ella hacía cualquier cosa.

Pues una mañana, muy de mañana, se levantó y nos dijo:

—¡Vamos! Vamos hijitos pa La Pintada.

La Pintada está a cuarenta y cinco millas de aquí [Sena]. De allá era ella más antes. De suerte es que salimos en la mañana. Vino y nos hizo prender los caballos y nos juimos.

Teníanos un caballo que le dijíanos el Pela [Perla], muy amachón. Era un caballo tan amachón que nomás llegaba a una cuestecita y ahi está el caballo apalancao patrás. Güeno. Llegamos a la orilla del pie de la vereda de Villanueva. En esos antonces era camino nomás de carros. Y esa cuesta era cuesta muy, muy, pus, era too punta pa subir. Estaba muy mala.

Cuando llegamos al pie de la vereda, destendió la mamá la vista pallá, parriba de Los Voladeros. Aá en la mera cumbre de Los Voladeros más alto, ahi estaba una viejita asina [encogida], como a las cinco, las seis de la mañana. La alcanzaba a ver ahi.

—Miren hijitos lo que está allá. Allá en la ladera, en Los Voladeros allá—aquí nomás que empiezas a subir la vereda, la ladera, aá en Los Voladeros—. Y ya nos dijo ella,

—Ni volteen paá, hijitos. ¡Vamos!

El caballo costumbraba que nomás llegábanos aá y se amachaba. Ese día solo subió, como quien dice, la cuesta. No se amachó ni naa. Cuarenta y cinco millas de ahi allá juimos. Pa las dos de la tarde estábanos en La Pintada. Cuando llegamos le platicó mamá a su papá la tragedia, ¿ves? Nosotros estábanos medianos. ¿Qué nos importaba tampoco como nada? Pus sin embargo que le platicó ella a su papá, el viejito, mi agüelo. Ya le dijo,

—¡Oh! ¡Son las brujas de Villanueva!

Pablo Aguilar

They're the Witches from Villanueva!

*O*n another occasion, this is what happened. It happened to me and to my mother and to my brother, there in Villanueva. Well, my stepfather was accustomed to going to work as usual, and my mother was of such demeanor that for her there was no such thing as a mishap. She was capable of doing just about anything.

Well, one morning, very early in the morning, she got up and she said to us:

"Let's go! Let's head for La Pintada, my dear children."

La Pintada is 45 miles from here [Sena]. That's where she was from a long time ago. It's a good thing we left in the morning. Anyway, she came and made us hitch up the horses and we took off.

We had a horse we used to call Pela [Perla], very stubborn. Boy, he was such a stubborn horse that no sooner he got to a little-bitty hill and there he was, holding back. We got to the foot of the hill, that is, the Villanueva trail. At that time it was a road only for horse wagons. And that hill was, well, it was straight up. It was very dangerous.

When we got to the foot of the trail, Mom looked on up ahead, up towards a place called Los Voladeros. Way up at the peak of the tallest of Los Voladeros, there was this little old lady like so [hunched up], at about five, six o'clock in the morning. My mother could see her.

"Look at what's there, kids. There on the hillside. Just about where the trail starts up the hill, there toward Los Voladeros." And about that time she said to us:

"Don't look that way, kids. Let's go!"

The horse was used to holding back whenever we got to that slope. On that particular day he climbed it like it was nothing. He didn't hold back or anything. We went 45 miles from there over to La Pintada. By two o'clock in the afternoon we were already in La Pintada. When we got there she spoke to her father about the mishap. You see? We [the children] were very small. What did we care about anything? Well, nevertheless, she told her father, my grandpa about it.

"Oh," he said to her. "They're the witches from Villanueva!"

Pablo Aguilar

25

Y ahi se acabó. Lo que tuvo más que ver, jue que el caballo no se amachó ese día. Y siempre íbanos temprano, pa agarrar suficiente tiempo pa subir. Y ese día, ya te digo, pa las dos de la tarde, ya estábanos en La Pintada.

Ésa es cosa comprobada que yo mismo la vide. Y me mande Dios un castigo si no es verdá.

And that's the end of the story. The most important thing is that the horse did not refuse to climb the hill on that particular day. And we always used to take off early in order to have enough time to climb that slope. And on that day, as I say, by two o'clock in the afternoon, we were already in La Pintada.

The incident is something I can vouch for because I saw it myself, with my own eyes. And may God punish me if it isn't true.

Pablo Aguilar

Anita U. Baca

ANITA U. BACA

Nació: El 5 de abril, 1905
Lobato, NM
Entrevista: El 1 de agosto, 1989
Lobato, NM
Fallecida

Born: April 5, 1905
Lobato, NM
Interview: August 1, 1989
Lobato, NM
Deceased

Tecolotes

Dicían que ahi onde jugaban a las muñecas las brujas, tenían encanto ahi. Oyí decir, no sé. Yo nunca vide, pero mis papás platicaban. Pus ya eran viejitos, muy viejitos. Y había muncho antes de brujos. Historias. Mis padres platicaban que es que hasta bailaban [las brujas]. Hacían monos, quizás, y aquí bajaban al Valle. Hacían mal en esos lugares. Sus brujerías. Eso oía yo dijir. Yo no sé.

Cuando estaba en papá malo, habían munchos tecolotes, y una viejita aquí en Villanueva era comadre de pila d'en papá. Muy poco vinía a velo; cuasi nunca vinía a velo. Yo y Gregorita López, mi sobrina, yo y ella nos manteníanos juntas chiquitas, y una vez vino esa viejita a casa de papá, y le dijimos,

—¿Pus qué tiene en esa rodilla? ¿Por qué tiene esas rodillas tan fieras?

—Pus nada hijita—dijía—. Nada. Me cayí.

Pero dijían que era bruja. Tenía unas rodillas murre fieras, pa todos rumbos, como que le daban pedradas en las piernas.

Y loo cuando se enfermó mi papá, pus no había venido a velo ella. ¡Ni una vez! Y un día cuando vinía mi hermano de allá de la borrega, antonces se respaldó allí en una sombra a descansar, y loo lo alcanzó a ver ella. Loo es que le dice ella,

—¡Vete! ¡Vete seguido! Tu papá se está muriendo.

Sin vinir ella a velo mientras estaba enfermo. Y era verdá. En papá estaba muy malo antonces. Otro día murió él.

Pero nojotros oíanos tecolotes en las zoteas todas las noches. Todas las noches. Y nunca pudimos apedrear niuno que bullía. Pus, ¿quién sabe?

Otra mujer, dijían munchas, que hacía a su marido tocar la guitarra estando colgada. Que le dijía ella,—Toca esta pieza—y es que la tocaba onde estaba colgada. No nos platicaba en papá porque eran compadres ellos. Nos platicaba mi mamá. Pero otras gentes nos platicaron lo mesmo después.

Anita U. Baca

Owls

People claimed that there, where the witches used to play dolls, that that's where they had their enchanted place. That's what I heard, I don't know. I never saw anything, but my dad and mom used to talk about that. They were quite old, very old. There was a lot of talk about witches a long time ago. All kinds of stories. My parents used to say that the witches would even dance. The witches would make like rag dolls, I guess, and they would come down here to the Valley and they'd do evil things all around these places. It was their sorcery. That's what I used to hear. I don't know if it's true.

When Dad was ill, there were lots of owls. And there was a little old lady here in Villanueva who was a *comadre* with the same first name as my dad's. She rarely ever came to visit him; she hardly ever came to see him. I and Gregorita López, my niece, we always hung around together when we were small, and one time this little old lady came here to my dad's house, and we said to her:

"Well, what is it you have on your knee? Why do you have such ugly knees?"

"Why nothing hijita," she would say. "Nothing. I fell down."

But people claimed that she was a witch. She had very ugly knees, which pointed in every direction, as if her legs had been stoned.

And then when my dad became ill, why, she had not come to see him. Not one time! One day when my brother was on his way back from herding sheep, he found a shady place to rest. When she managed to spot him, she said to him:

"Shake a leg! Get going quickly! Your dad's dying."

She knew without having gone to see him. And it was true. Dad was very ill at the time. He died the next day.

But we used to hear owls every night on top of the roofs. Every night. And we were never even able to hit even one of the hooting owls with a rock [owls are a bad omen and sometimes are harbingers of death]. Well, who knows?

There was another woman, so claimed many people, who could make her husband play the guitar while it was hanging on the wall. She would say to him, "Play this number," and I understand the guitar played by itself. My dad didn't tell us anything about it because they (the lady and the father) were *compadres*. It was our mom who would tell us the story. But later on other people also told us the same thing.

Anita U. Baca

Celia Benavídez

CELIA BENAVÍDEZ

Nació: El 13 de abril, 1910
San Juan, NM
Entrevista: El 7 de junio, 1990
Ancón, NM

Born: April 13, 1910
San Juan, NM
Interview: June 7, 1990
Ancón, NM

Un hombre en un burrito blanco

Pues éste era mi *granpo*. Él vinía en un caballo de San Miguel, y en frente del camposanto de San José topó un hombre en un burrito blanco, y él vistido tamién de blanco. Ya serían como las doce. Quién sabe si se pasaban. El caballo que traiba mi *granpo*, pues, se espantó cuando lo sintió, pero el hombre este pasó en el burrito y le dio las güenas noches.

Al siguiente año, tocó que mi papá estaba aprendiendo a músico con el dijunto Juan García, que tocaba violín. Antonces vinía él a la misma hora que le salió a su suegro este burrito con este hombre vistido de blanco, en el mismo lugar. Pero nomás eso le hablaba. Nomás las güenas noches le daba. Cerca del camposanto de San José.

Es que era un ánima que andaba penando, pero no hizo ningún mal. El caballo sí se espantó porque era muy de repente, pero no le hizo nada.

34

Una señora vistida de amarillo

Yo vivía en San Juan cuando estaba muy joven. Nosotros viníanos a San José por una vereda. Pa no troviar el camino, subíanos derecho a un lugar que le dicían Los Banquitos. Vinimos al baile con un tío, yo y otra prima.

De aquí pallá cuando íbanos, que íbanos a pie por el mismo lugar, vimos una señora parada, vistida de amarillo, con el cabello todo pa la cara, cabello largo. A nosotros nos dio muncho temor, muncho miedo. Nos agarramos del tío, cada una del brazo, pero esta señora iba voltiando. Conforme nosotros que íbanos caminando, ella iba voltiando con la cara pa onde estábanos nosotros, pero no se le vía cara. Nomás el puro cabello.

Nosotros no la oímos llorar. Nomás la vimos, pero vistida de amarillo.

Celia Benavídez

A Man on a Little White Donkey

*T*his is a story about my grandpa. He was riding on horseback from San Miguel, and in front of the cemetery in San José he ran into a man on a little white donkey. The man was also dressed in white. It must have been about twelve o'clock at night, perhaps later. The horse that my grandpa had, well, it got scared when he sensed the man on the white donkey, but all this man did was to say goodnight as he went by on his donkey.

The following year, it so happens that my dad was learning how to be a musician with the late Juan García, who played the violin. My dad was headed home and at the same hour and the same place the donkey and the man dressed in white reappeared. But all the man would say was to bid him goodnight. This was close to the San José cemetery.

It was supposedly a soul that was roaming in sorrow, but it didn't do any harm. The horse did get scared because it happened so suddenly, but the soul or spirits didn't do anything to him.

35

A Woman Dressed in Yellow

I used to live in San Juan when I was very young. We used to go to San José on a trail. In order not to miss the road, we would go straight up a place they used to call Los Banquitos. Once we went to the dance—an uncle, a cousin, and I.

On the way back, as we were walking down the same place, we saw a woman standing, dressed in yellow, with her long hair all over her face. My cousin and I got really frightened, very scared. We grabbed ahold of our uncle, one on each arm, but this woman kept turning. As we continued walking, she kept turning with her face in the direction where we were, but you couldn't see her face. Only her hair.

We never heard her cry. All we did was see her dressed in yellow.

Celia Benavídez

¡Tan linda!

Nosotros vivíanos en un rancho. Yo tenía una hermana que estaba más grande que yo. Nosotros visitábanos muncho a una señora que se llamaba Juanita. Y esta señora tenía un nieto, y ella estaba interesada de que mi hermana se casara con él. Y mi hermana, pus ella no quiso.

El cuento es que esta mujer la abrazó y le dijo,—¡Tan linda!—y le pegó un beso en un cachete. En poco tiempo resultó que a mi hermana le salió un grano, y con nada descansaba. Y luego yo que era la más mediana le dije a mi papá,

—Doña Juana besó a mi hermana.

Antonces él dijo,

—Esta señora me la paga.

Agarró un cabresto y se jue y le dijo,

—Ora me curas a m'hija y si no este cabresto no te ha parido.

Y le dio un remedio ella. No sé qué sería. Yo estaba muy joven. Puede que yo tuviera como unos once años. Y con ese remedio nomás se lo untó y descansó.

La señora estaba nojada porque no quiso mi hermana casarse con el nieto.

Celia Benavídez

So Beautiful!

We used to live on a ranch. I had a sister who was older than me. We would visit this woman a lot whose name was Juanita. And this woman had a grandson, and she was interested in having him marry my sister. And my sister, well, she just didn't want to.

And so the story goes that this woman hugged her and said to her, "So beautiful!," and kissed her on one of her cheeks. Soon my sister developed a boil, and it didn't matter what it was treated with, she couldn't get well. And since I was the youngest I said to my dad:

"Doña Juana kissed my sister."

Then he said, "I'll get even with this woman."

He grabbed a rope and he took off and he said to her, "You either get my daughter well or you'll find yourself at the end of this rope."

So she gave her a remedy. I don't know what it was. I was very young. I must have been about 11 years old. All my sister did was to rub that remedy on herself and she got well.

37

The woman was angry because my sister refused to marry her grandson.

Celia Benavídez

Vieron ir una brasa

Mi marido y mi tío vinían de su trabajo en carro de bestias, y sestiaron de aquel lao de Tecolote. Ahi iban a dormir. Y en eso que estaban cenando, vieron ir una brasa del rumbo del Tecolote. Cuando salieron, mi tío sacó un rifle y cartuchos y le tiró un balazo. Le pegó. Se desbarató.

Otro día, que salieron pal rumbo del Tecolote, se pararon a platicar con unos amigos. Y ahi les platicaron que esta señora se había caído de una escalera en la noche y se había lastimado. Tenía un golpe. Estaban en esa crencia de que era el balazo que él le había dado mi tío. Se murió.

En otra vez era en el verano, y una señora que vivía aquí en San José en una casa vieja, no estaba aquí en casa. Ella estaba en Bernalillo. Y esta señora vinía siendo tía de mi suegra. Una noche nos salimos ajuera yo y mi suegra a tomar fresco. Ya estábanos poco esparciando.

Era en el verano, como le digo, cuando vimos que estaban saliendo como brasas del chiflón del fogón mexicano. Al rato ya vimos que salió una brasa y voló pa la zotea, cuando antonces usábanos techos de antes. Eran zoteas. Y de ahi brincó pa bajo, y esta brasa se apagaba y se prendía.

Y de ahi voló a unos corrales viejos. Y ahi en esos corrales vinía la luna—porque hay una loma. La luna no se vía todavía. En aquella sombra, ahi se despareció. No supimos qué pasó con ella.

Pues dicían que era una bruja, pero no sé. La mujer no estaba aquí en casa.

Celia Benavídez

They Saw a Fireball Go By

My husband and my uncle were coming home from work in a horse wagon, and they stopped to rest on the other side of Tecolote. That's where they were going to sleep. About the time they were eating supper, they saw a fireball go by in the direction of Tecolote. When they came out, my uncle grabbed a rifle and some shells and fired a shot at it. He hit it, and it disintegrated.

Next day, as they headed for Tecolote, they stopped to talk with some friends. That's where they were told that this woman had fallen from a ladder the night before and had gotten hurt. She had a bump on her. They thought for sure that it was the bullet that my uncle had fired that had hit her. The woman died.

Another time, it was summertime, and this woman lived in an old house here in San José, but she wasn't home. She was in Bernalillo. As it turns out, this woman was my mother-in-law's aunt. One night my mother-in-law and I went outside to get some fresh air. We were already a little relaxed.

As I say, it was in the summer, when all of a sudden we saw what appeared to be sparks (ashes) coming from the pot-bellied stove's chimney. A little while later we saw a spark fly onto the roof. This was at a time when we had old-fashioned roofs, flat roofs. From there it jumped down, and this spark would light up and then disappear.

From there it flew to some old corrals. There from those corrals, the moon would come up from behind a hill. You couldn't see the moon yet. In that shadow, that's where the spark disappeared. We never did find out what happened to it.

People used to say that it was a witch. I don't know, but the woman wasn't home.

Celia Benavídez

Isidora M. Flores

ISIDORA M. FLORES

Nació: El 9 de octubre, 1910
Villanueva, NM
Entrevista: El 31 de mayo, 1989
Villanueva, NM

Born: October 9, 1910
Villanueva, NM
Interview: May 31, 1989
Villanueva, NM

41

No pescaron la bruja

*L*as curanderas de las brujas, más antes, eso era el chiste que oía yo. Que toavía muncha gente creiba en ellas. Que ondequiera que iba, que te digo yo, que creiban en las brujas. Muncha gente ponía abujas hechas cruz en las ventanas, en las puertas. Isque no entraban las brujas.

Y otra cosa, que isque si te mordía un perro, no te hacían nada las brujas. Y luego, mi mamá me dicía que a los Juanes no les hacen nada las brujas. Onde hay un Juan o una Juana no entran las brujas.

Y a mi mamá le pasó un chasco cuando estaba un tío viejito, hermanito de mi agüelito. Es que tenía un grano, yo creo que era cáncer, en la lengua. Le dijían que era brujería. Y isque que se juntaban perros a aullar, y tecolotes, y la gente vía visiones y qué sabe qué tanto. Yo no sé. Mamá toavía platicaba que era verdá.

Pus, la pusieron a mamá y a una vecina Juana, onde estaba el enfermo pa que entrara la bruja, porque se ponía muy mal el tío viejito, de medianoche pa delante. Iban a pescala la bruja cuando llegaba. Y dice mamá que taparon la ventana con almuadas. Pusieron almuadas una arriba de la otra, y cuando se llegó a medianoche se cayó una de las almuadas de arriba a abajo. ¡Se espantó la Juana y no pescaron la bruja!

Estaban los hombres con rifles y too allá fuera. Isque aullaban los perros. Que se oían ruidos. No sé por qué. No sé si sería verdá. Pero al tío viejito lo sanó una curandera de por ahi de Sena.

Isidora M. Flores

They Didn't Catch the Witch

The women folk healers cured the witches' doings of long ago, that was the joke I used to hear. A lot of people still believed in them. Wherever I went, people believed in witches. Many people would put needles in the form of crosses on the windows, on the doors. Word has it that the witches wouldn't go in.

And another thing, if a dog bit you, the witches couldn't harm you. And then, my mom told me that the witches won't inflict any harm on those named Juan, that wherever there's a Juan or a Juana, the witches won't go in.

My mom had a bad experience when an old uncle, my grandpa's brother, was around. I understand he had a sore, I believe it was cancer, on his tongue. People used to tell him that it was caused by witchcraft. Rumor has it that dogs would gather and howl—owls gathered also—and people saw visions and who knows what all. I don't know. Mom said that it was true; she talked for a long time as though it were true.

Well, they put Mom and a neighbor named Juana where the sick man was so that the witch would come in, from midnight on, because the uncle would get very ill. They were going to catch the witch whenever she got there. And Mom says that they covered the window with pillows. They stacked the pillows one on top of the other, and when midnight came one of the pillows fell down from the top of the heap. The Juana got startled and they didn't catch the witch!

The men were ready outside with rifles and everything. I understand the dogs were howling. Noises could be heard. I don't know why. I don't know if it was true or not.

But the old uncle was cured by a folk healer from around Sena.

Isidora M. Flores

Iba la cabra volando

Mi tío Toribio, hermanito de mi *Dad*, platicaba unas historias terribles de las brujas. Que una vez andaba él en Colorao, trabajando, y loo había llegao una mujer y que le había dicho él:

—Yo quiero ir pa mi casa al baile—isque le dijo.

—Si me prometes volver pa medianoche, yo te llevo.

Aquí en Villanueva era el baile. Y loo isque le dijo él:

—Sí. Sí te prometo volver. Nomás quiero ir a dar güelta.

Y era el casorio de alguien. Pos que lo subió en una cabra, la mujer esta. Isque le dijo:

—Sin Dios y sin Santa María.

Y él como en un sueño que iba la cabra volando. En un *instant* estuvo en el baile.

Y loo cuando salió del baile, tenía que dijir esas mesmas palabras: "Sin Dios y sin Santa María." Y dice que se le aprontó la cabra y se volvió a subir en la cabra. Eran las once y media, y voló pa Colorao.

Bueno, yo no sé si sería historia dél, pero [como] le digo, había munchos chistes de las brujas.

44

Isidora M. Flores

The Goat Was Flying

My uncle Toribio, my dad's younger brother, used to tell some horrible stories about witches. Once upon a time he was in Colorado, working, when a woman showed up, whereupon he said to her, "I want to go back home to a dance."

"If you promise to return by midnight, I'll take you," she said to him.

The dance was here in Villanueva. He said to her, "Yes. I promise to return as you suggest. I just want to go make the rounds."

It was somebody's wedding.

Well, I understand this woman propped him on top of a goat, and she said to him, "Without God and without Saint Mary."

He was like in a dream. The goat was like flying. In just an instant he was at the dance.

Then when he left the dance, he had to say those same words: "Without God and without Saint Mary." And as he said that, the goat suddenly appeared and he hopped on it once again. It was eleven-thirty when the goat flew back to Colorado.

Now, I don't know if it was a story that he made up, but I'm telling you, there were lots of jokes about witches.

45

Isidora M. Flores

Fortunato G. Gallegos and Frances F. Gallegos

FORTUNATO G. GALLEGOS

Nació: El 16 de enero, 1917
Villanueva, NM
Entrevista: El 17 de julio, 1992
Villanueva, NM

Born: January 16, 1917
Villanueva, NM
Interview: July 17, 1992
Villanueva, NM

Entierros

Me acuerdo de un viejito que nos espantaba cuando teníanos las borregas. Se llamaba Severo Chávez. ¿Ha oido usted en inglés de *A Thousand and One Nights*? Viene de la España, de la Alhambra. Él las contaba toas. Cada noche contaba una de *Las mil y una noches*. Y ese viejito seguro que no sabía ni ler, pero se las pasaban los viejitos unos a los otros.

Me acuerdo que dijían que había entierros en algunas casas. Toavía ora dicen que eran de nuestros primeros antepasados, que ahi vinieron a enterrar ellos porque es que había gentes aá alrededor y eran muy tenidos. No, no gustaba el dinero, y hacían dinero. Que no saben qué harían con él. Que quizá lo dejaran enterrao ahi porque había como alguno de ésos que vendían munchos animales. Vendían vacas y vendían caballos y too. Y no sabían qué hacían con el dinero porque, pus, no necesitaban de comprar nada. Too, too lo cosechaban aquí. Y figuraban que aquí está el dinero too por ahi. Y munchos dicen que la gente que vivía antes, que no creían en el dinero de papel, pior cuando entraron los Estaos Unidos. Que ya no querían dinero, [no] sonaban la plata o onzas de oro. Que dejaron su dinero enterrao munchos. Munchos viejitos no le dicían ni a la mujer, yo creo. Pero yo no creo en eso.

Eran cuentos. Aquí con un tío mío, este tío que vivía aquí en San Antonio, compró un atajo de casas viejas que estaban juntas ahi y hizo un salón. Y tenía un viejito trabajando ahi, tirando las casas, y el viejito se halló una ollita con dinero, ¿ve? Y el pobrecito era muy humilde, y vino y se lo trujo a mi tío, y es que no le dio ni un pene mi tío. Y creo que sí porque estuvo muy golozo mi tío por muncho tiempo.

Yo no me acuerdo de ese tiempo, pero ya hacía poco que [yo] estaba aquí [en el mundo]. Era como mil nuevecientos diez y siete, yo creo.

48

Fortunato G. Gallegos

Buried Treasures

I remember a little old man who used to scare us during the time we raised sheep. His name was Severo Chávez. Have you heard in English of *A Thousand and One Nights*? It comes from Spain, from the Alhambra [Granada]. He used to relate all of those stories. Every night he would tell us one. And for sure that little old man didn't know how to read, but the old folks would pass the stories from one to another.

I remember people saying that there were buried treasures in some houses. Even now people say that our forefathers dared to bury treasures because there were individuals around who were very bold. They didn't seek pleasure from money, but they made money. Who knows what they did with it? Perhaps they left it buried somewhere, like some of those people who would sell a lot of animals. They'd sell cattle and horses and everything. And people didn't know what they did with the money because, well, they didn't need to buy anything. They raised or harvested everything right here. So people figured that the money was hidden somewhere around here. And there are those who say that the people of yesteryear didn't believe in paper money, and this feeling became even more serious when we became part of the United States. People no longer wanted paper money; they no longer wanted to make noises with silver and gold coins either. That is why many of them buried their money. Many of the little old men didn't even tell their wives about the money, I guess. But I don't believe in that.

They were just tales. Like with one of my uncles here, this uncle who lived in San Antonio, who bought a bunch of old houses that were all strung together. He built a saloon. And he had an old man there working for him, knocking down the houses, and the old man found a small pan full of money. You see? And the poor old man was very meek, and he went and took it to my uncle, and I understand that my uncle didn't even give him a penny as a reward. I believe that's true because he, my uncle, became very greedy for a long time. I don't recall that particular time period, but I had already been on this earth for a little while. I believe it was around 1917 or so.

Fortunato G. Gallegos

49

Amaneció una mujer muerta

Más antes de mis tiempos sí es que eran [la gente] muy supersticiosos. Vían luces en las casas que no había lámparas de como eléctricas. Vían como cuando hacía un relámpago. Es que se quedaba la luz y oían quejidos adentro la casa. Eran muy supersticiosos.

El coco siempre estaba. Dicían que si éranos malcriaos que ahi vinía el coco, vinía el agüelo y con chicote los [nos] arreglaba. Y si se portaba uno mal, se le podía aparecer.

Lo que platicaban aquí, que había un hombre, que quizás era amigo muy valiente y vivía aá junto el atarque. Y vinía pacá pa la Plaza y se celebraba, seguro, ¿ve? Y es que una noche pasaba por una casa vieja que estaba allí. Ya nomás las paredes estaban ahi. Y es que vio muncha luz adentro, como que había gente adentro, y agarró una piedra y tiró pa dentro y que oyó un quejido y se apagaron las luces. ¿Ve? Y otro día es que amaneció una mujer muerta aquí [en Villanueva].

Ésas eran las historias que platicaban de ese hombre. Que era un hombre que se llamaba Prada. Y que era muy valiente. Tiró una pedrada pa dentro de la ventana. No tenía ventanas la casa ni nada. Era una casa vieja, abandonada, y oyó un quejido quizás cuando le conetó piedra de aquí. Ellos [la gente] crían que vían algo, ¿no?

50

Fortunato G. Gallegos

A Woman Was Found Dead

*L*ong ago before my time I guess people were very superstitious. They would see lights in homes where there were no electric lamps. They'd see lights like when lightning strikes. It is said that the lights would stay on and people would also hear moaning inside the house. They were pretty superstitious.

The bogeyman was always around. They would tell us that if we misbehaved the bogeyman would come, the *agüelo* would come and straighten us out with a whip. If you disobeyed, he could appear.

What people talked about around here is that there was a man, who perhaps was a pretty courageous fellow, who lived close to the dam. And he'd come to the Plaza and have a few drinks. People say that one night he was going by this old house that used to be there. Only the walls were still standing. And he saw a lot of light inside and there were people inside. He grabbed a rock and tossed it inside, and about that time he heard a moan and then the lights went out. And the next day a woman was found dead here in Villanueva.

Those were the stories people told about that man whose name was Prada. And he was very brave. He threw a rock through the window part of the house. The house had no windows or anything. It was an old, abandoned house, and the man I guess heard a moan when he connected with the rock. People thought they saw something, right?

51

Fortunato G. Gallegos

Isabel Gallegos

ISABEL GALLEGOS

Nació: El 16 de abril, 1909
La Fragua, NM
Entrevista: El 8 de octubre, 1993
Garambullo, NM

Born: April 16, 1909
La Fragua, NM
Interview: October 8, 1993
Garambullo, NM

Metían miedo los viejos

Algunos dicían que había brujas. Algunos viejos platicaban que había brujas. Nos dicía mi agüelo, el dijunto Lorenzo, bisagüelo, que tuviéranos cuidao que el diablo andaba, y las brujas tamién, que no juéranos agarrar esto o lotro, que lo vieran las brujas. Algún regalo que dicen.

Pues dicían que las brujas se volvían brasas, que se volvían tecolotes, liones, o de todos modos, y hasta diablos, seguro, porque era cómo pasa. Y era que las había.

¡Oh no! No la quiero, la cosa mala. Y la Llorona, pues, no era más que una mujer que le tenía miedo la gente en México. En un puente que estaba, esta mujer lloraba nomás. Le pusieron la Llorona, que al fin la agarraron. No la vían. Pueda que juera bruja. La gente le tenía muncho miedo al pasar ese puente. Sería bruja, ¿quién sabe? Pus la gente o alguna persona la pescó. Quién sabe qué harían con ella. La quitarían del medio. O la dejaron a que no volviera a temorizar a la gente.

Yo sí creía en el agüelo y el coco. Metían miedo los viejos. Casi no me acuerdo muy bien pero se ponían máscaras y nos metían miedo a que no juéranos a malcriar. Con un chicote te agarraban.

54

Isabel Gallegos

The Old Folks Would Scare You

Some people used to say that there were witches around, especially the old folks. My grandpa, the late Lorenzo, who was really my great-grandfather, used to tell us to be careful with the devil who was loose—the witches also—and not to go accept this or that because the witches might have cast a spell on it. For example some gift or something.

Well, people claimed that witches could turn into ashes, or into owls, lions, or just about anything, even into the devil, because that's just the way it was. And that's because there were witches around.

Oh no! I don't want any evil spirits. And the Wailing Woman, well, she was only a woman people in Mexico were afraid of. There was this bridge, and there'd be this woman crying. They named it the Wailing Woman, who was finally captured. They couldn't see her. Perhaps she was a witch. The people were very scared of her as they crossed that bridge. Could it have been a witch, who knows? Well, some people or somebody did catch her. Who knows what they did with her. Maybe they did away with her. Or they left her in such a state that she would not torment people anymore.

Yes, I believed in the *agüelo* or the bogeyman. That's how the old folks would scare you. I don't recall very well, but they'd put on masks or they would catch us with a whip to scare us so we wouldn't misbehave.

Isabel Gallegos

Josephine M. Gallegos

JOSEPHINE M. GALLEGOS

Nació: El 30 de noviembre, 1915
Villanueva, NM
Entrevista: El 9 de febrero, 1996
Villanueva, NM

Born: November 30, 1915
Villanueva, NM
Interview: February 9, 1996
Villanueva, NM

Tenía la viejita un chivato

Una vez, mi tío Toribio, que estaba en Colorao él en el betabel, nos platicaba una historia. Se iba a casar alguien aquí en Villanueva. Él quería malamente vinir al baile. También es que conocía él a una viejita. Es que le dijo la viejita,

—Si quieres ir al baile, yo te llevo, pero tienes que estar listo pa golver pa las doce de la noche.

—Bueno—es que le dijo él.

Y le cobró tanto ella. Temprano jueron, y tenía la viejita, quizás, un chivato, por aá ajuera. Es que lo hizo subir en el chivato y ella con él.

—Cuando nos súbanos—le dijo ella—tienes que dijir, 'Sin Dios y Santa María.'

Se subieron y jueron a dar al baile. Y antes del baile isque le dijo ella otra vez,

—Cuando salgas tienes que golver a dijir 'Sin Dios y Santa María' y te traigo patrás.

Y golvieron hacer la misma, y golvieron patrás en tiempo, y ahi se acabó la historia.

58

Josephine M. Gallegos

The Little Old Lady Had a Billy Goat

*O*nce upon a time my uncle Toribio, who was in Colorado work-ing in the beet fields, was telling us a story. Someone was going to get married here in Villanueva, whom he knew, and he wanted to come to the dance very badly. He knew a little old lady who sup-posedly said to him:

"If you wish to go to the dance, I'll take you, but you have to be ready to return by twelve o'clock at night."

"Very well," he responded.

And she charged him so much money. They were ready to go quite early and the little old lady had a billy goat, I guess, somewhere outside. She made him get on the billy goat and she got on as well.

"When we hop on," she said to him, "you have to say, 'Without God and Saint Mary.'"

They got on the billy goat and just like that they were at the dance. And before the dance started she said to him once again:

"When you leave the dance, once again you must say 'Without God and Saint Mary' and I'll take you back home."

They did the same thing upon return, and they returned on time, and that's the end of the story.

Josephine M. Gallegos

Lala Gallegos

LALA GALLEGOS

Nació: El 7 de mayo, 1927
Villanueva, NM
Entrevista: El 22 de agosto, 1989
Villanueva, NM
Fallecida

Born: May 7, 1927
Villanueva, NM
Interview: August 22, 1989
Villanueva, NM
Deceased

Supersticiones

El hombre que andaba era bien parecido, y que toas las mujeres andaban en pues dél. Y luego pus fue y sacó a una muchacha a bailar, y al rato que andaban bailando, quién sabe cómo vido la muchacha patrás y le vido la cola. Loo vido pa bajo y le vido las pezuñas. Antonces se espantó la muchacha y lo dejó y se traquió. Pegó un traquido y se despareció. Era la cosa mala.

_ _ _

Había un hombre que iba a ver a la novia. Y ahi onde iba en el camino, oyó llorar un bebito y se jue al llorido del bebito, y lo jalló. Y lo levantó y se subió en el caballo con él. Cuando se subió en el caballo, le dijo el bebito,

—¡Mira, tata, ya tengo dientes!

Antonces jue cuando le vido los dientes al bebito y jondió al bebito y se jue y no más golvió a ver a la novia de noche. De día sí, pero de noche no.

_ _ _

Éste era un vecino que teníanos nojotros. Venía a la medianoche de jugar _pool_. Aquí mismo en este lugar, en Villanueva, venía cuando venía en frente de en casa, papá vido pasar una lumbre muy juerte en un lao del vecino. Era una bola de lumbre. Y papá reclama que no era otra cosa más que una bruja la que pasó por un lao del vecino. Y no más golvió andar jugando _pool_ hasta medianoche, ni salir en la noche. Ésas eran brujas, dicen, que brincaban las lumbres de un lao de la 'cequia pa lotro, aquí mismo en Villanueva.

_ _ _

Había una viejita vecina que vivía aquí en estos arededores. Pus se sentaba en un cajón, y otra viejita que venía a pasearse vía que nunca se levantaba la viejita del cajón. Una vez cuando se levantó se asomó al cajón la otra viejita a ver qué había, la que vino a visitar, y vido que era una pila de lagartijos los que estaban adentro. Y

Lala Gallegos

Superstitions

This man who ran around was a good-looking man, and all of the women were after him. And then he went and asked a young lady to dance and shortly after they started dancing, by chance the girl happened to look behind him and saw a tail and saw that he also had hoofs. Then the girl got scared and left him, and suddenly there was a cracking noise. The cracking noise sounded loud and he disappeared. It was the evil spirits.

⚘ ⚘ ⚘

There was this man who was on his way to visit his girlfriend. And on the way, he heard a baby crying and headed in that direction, and he found him. He picked him up and got on the horse with him. When he got on the horse, the baby said to him:

"Look, daddy, I already have teeth!"

It was then that he saw the baby's teeth, and he tossed the baby down and took off and he never again went to see his girlfriend at night. During the day, yes, but not at night.

⚘ ⚘ ⚘

This is the story about a neighbor that we had. It was late at night when he was on his way home from playing pool. It happened right here in Villanueva, and on his way home right in front of our house, Dad saw a very strong light go by next to our neighbor. It was a ball of fire. And Dad claims that it was none other than a witch who passed by the neighbor. And he never ever again played pool late at night, let alone go out at night. Those balls of fire that jumped from one side of the ditch to the other, right here in Villanueva, were witches, according to some people

⚘ ⚘ ⚘

There was a little old lady, a neighbor, who used to live around these parts. She was in the habit of sitting on a wooden crate, and another little old lady who came to visit her from time to time saw that her neighbor almost never got up from the wooden crate. But one time when the little old lady got up, the other lady took a peek

Lala Gallegos

eso era algo con que ella hacía los males, entiendo yo, con los puros lagartijos onde se sentaba ahi en el cajoncito. Eso es verdá.

≈ ≈ ≈

Y de brujas, esto le pasó tamién a otra mujer. Es que le hicieron la brujería por las flores. Y eran de escenario (decoración). Y no aquí en Novo México, pero en otro lugar, la curó esta curandera y le dijo que sabía quién era la persona que la mantenía enferma todo el tiempo a ella. Le dijo que con una bandeja con agua que iba saber quién era la que le había hecho el mal. Y la dejó cuidando la bandeja con agua, y resultó una mota de un escenario con la agua. Antonces supo la enferma la que le había hecho el mal en las flores de la ventana. Se le secaron las flores, y ahi salió el escenario. Antonces se acordó ella, pero ya la persona que le había hecho el mal era muerta. Después levantaba flores, pero no se componían. No se componían. Le hizo el mal de las flores pa siempre. Y nunca pudo levantar flores de ventana. Adentro de la casa, no. Ajuera sí, pero adentro no.

≈ ≈ ≈

A esta mujer le hicieron mal pero no sabía en qué. Jue a que la curaran y la curó la médica y le dijo que no sabía quién le había hecho el mal, pero que la iba a curar. No le podía dijir el nombre de la persona, pero que cuando ella echara algo fiero iba saber quién le había hecho el mal. Entonces le dio basca y echó una pila de plumas de gallina. Antonces se acordó de la persona que le hizo el mal.

≈ ≈ ≈

Yo sí le hice ojo a un muchito, pero el ojo se cura muy fácil, si lo agarran en tiempo. Si se pasa un viernes se muere el muchito. La persona responsable por el mal ojo lo cura si le da agua con la boca,

Lala Gallegos

inside the crate to see what there was, and she saw a bunch of lizards inside the box. That's what she used to inflict evil doings, so I understand, just by simply using the lizards in the small wooden crate where she sat. That's the truth.

⁂

And that business of witches, this also is what happened to another woman. They say that she was bewitched through her own flowers. The woman had them arranged in a bouquet of six. And this lady folk healer cured her, not here in New Mexico, but in another place, and she told her who the person was who had her in this state of perpetual illness. She told her that she would be able to tell who bewitched her just by putting water in a pan. The folk healer left her alone watching the pan of water, and six cotton balls showed up. Then the sick woman knew who had bewitched her using the flowers on the windowsill. The flowers dried up, and the figure six showed up. She remembered who the person who had bewitched her was, but she was already dead. Later on the woman would pick flowers, but they wouldn't last. The dead person had put an evil spell on the flowers forever. And the woman was never able to pick flowers and put them inside on the windowsill because they would dry up. Outside, yes, but not inside.

65

⁂

This is the story about a woman who was bewitched, but she didn't know where or why. She went to a female healer to be cured—and she was cured—but she didn't know who had cast an evil spell on her. The healer told her she couldn't tell her the name of the person who had bewitched her, but that she would cure her. In the process she would have a bowel movement and she would pass something unpleasant. Then she got nauseated and she passed a bunch of chicken feathers. The woman with the spell then remembered who it was who had bewitched her.

⁂

I myself did cast the evil eye on a little boy, but the evil eye can be cured very easily, if you catch it in time. If it goes beyond a Friday the little boy will die. The person responsible for casting the evil

Lala Gallegos

anque munchas personas dicen que no siempre es güeno. Pero pones tú un vaso con agua, abajo de la cunita del bebito, con un güevo en l'agua, y lo pones un popotito en el vaso. Todo lo pones abajo de la cunita del bebito onde está durmiendo. Si el güevo sube parriba, es que el bebito tiene ojo. Y si el güevo se queda en el plan, no tiene ojo. Pero si tiene ojo, antonces se cura el bebito con agua en la boca. Asina curé yo mi perrita, dos veces.

⚹ ⚹ ⚹

Y a otra mujer también le hicieron mal en el chile verde. Y se mantenía mala y mala y mala y bien panzona. La operaron y no le jallaron nada a esta mujer. Y loo jallaron este curandero y la curó con remedios y le dijo que cuando ella viera lo que echara, antonces iba ver el que le había hecho el mal. Y echó el chile verde fresco conforme lo había comido, siendo que no había comido chile verde. Pus ya el chile verde en que le había hecho mal era ya años y años pasaos. Y lo echó fresco, fresco, antonces. Antonces se acordó quién era la persona. Ése es verdá. Ése es la mera verdá.

⚹ ⚹ ⚹

Y loo hay gente que te hacen mal con los ojos. Si tú estás platicando con una persona que te tiene mala voluntá y tú no lo sabes, con los mismos ojos della te está viendo a ti, te está haciendo el mal. Y te hace mal, con los mismo ojos.

O en la noche. Hay unos polvos. Viene y te los echa en las puertas, quizás cuando ya tú estás acostada. Te los echa abajo en el piso de la puerta y loo tú sales en la mañana pa juera, o sea la noche después, y lo[s] levantas con el pie. Ya se te prenden. Ahi te hacen el mal pero tú no sabes.

No te comienza diuna vez. Se tarda uno, dos años pa comenzarte a trabajar. Para ese tiempo tu espíritu se te ha olvidao, ves, pero a aquella persona del maleficio no se le olvidó. No está esperando más que se te llegue el tiempo pa que sufras.

Lala Gallegos

eye alone can cure it by giving the afflicted baby water by mouth, although many people claim that it's not always good to do that. But you put a glass of water right underneath the baby's crib, with an egg in the glass of water, and then you place a small stalk or straw underneath on top of the glass. Everything has to be underneath the crib where the baby is sleeping. If the egg floats to the top, it's because the baby has the evil eye. And if the egg stays at the bottom, the baby doesn't have the evil eye.

The way to cure a little baby, if the egg floats to the top, is by giving it water by mouth. That's how I also cured my little dog, twice.

ﻬ ﻬ ﻬ

And there's another woman whose green chile was cursed. There she was sick, time and time again, and very bloated. They operated on her and found nothing. Then they found this folk healer, and he cured her with herbal remedies. He told her that once she saw what went through her biologically, then she would see who had cast the evil spell. And she discharged fresh green chile that she hadn't even eaten. It was in the chile that someone had cast a bad spell, years and years back. And it was fresh as could be. Then she remembered who the person was. That's the truth. That's the real truth.

ﻬ ﻬ ﻬ

Mean-spirited people can poison your food. They'll do it with their eyes. If you're talking to a person who's got it in for you and you don't know it, all she has to do is look at you with her eyes, and she's inflicting evil on you. And she'll do it, just by using her eyes.

Or at night. There are certain powders. She'll come and spread them at your doorstep, perhaps when you're already in bed. She'll spread them underneath the doormat and then you step outside the door in the morning, the night afterward, and you pick them [powders] up with your shoes. From then on you're stuck.

The malevolence doesn't start right away. It takes one or two years for the powders to begin to work. By that time your human spirit has forgotten about it, you see, but she [the evildoer] hasn't forgotten. All she's doing is waiting for the right time for the powders to take their course so that you begin to suffer.

Lala Gallegos

El hijo malcriao

Éste era el hijo muy malcriao, que no obedecía a su padre. Eso es verdá porque mi agüelita no[s] lo platicaba. Ella lo vido en aquellos tiempos cuando ella estaba muchacha.

El papá iba por un camino y el muchacho no quería. Y un día le dio coraje al hijo y le levantó la mano y al tiempo que la levantó pa pegale a su papá, se le secó la mano y al mesmo tiempo lo tragó la tierra, hasta la cintura.

Y luego la gente se puso a rezale y rezale a Dios y no lo podían sacar y loo empezaron a escarbar. Mientras más lo escarbaban, más abajo se iba, y lo estaba impidiendo muncho la tierra hasta que se secó de la cintura pa bajo.

Loo el hijo mesmo le prometió a Dios que si lo sacaba, él iba a andar de rodillas por el resto de su vida por las cuatro partes del mundo, predicando de Dios y lo que le había pasao con su padre, y predicando a otros hijos que no jueran malos con sus padres, que los obedecieran. Si no, les pasaba lo que le había pasao a él.

Después que Dios abrió la tierra y lo soltó, el hijo cumplió con su deber y anduvo las cuatro partes del mundo hasta que se murió.

A mí me han hecho tantos males

A mí me han hecho tantos [males] que unos de ellos sí están horrorosos. Dos han estao muy horrorosos, que cuasi me han mandao a la sepultura, pero güenos espíritus güelven patrás. Cuando ya me miran que estoy pa cae pa bajo me güelven y eso me pasó. No diré ónde, pero eso jue en 1950, que eché pura sangre de los pulmones por la boca.

Eché unos cuajarones de los pulmones! Me dio el dotor tres días pa vivir. ¡Tres días!

Me acuerdo que era día martes y logo día miércoles me jui a una médica, y logo el siguiente día me tenía que murir. Eso mismo me

Lala Gallegos

The Disobedient Son

This is the story about a very disobedient son who didn't obey his father. It's true because my grandma used to tell us about it. She saw it back when she was a girl.

The father used to head down this one road, but the boy didn't like it. One day the son got angry and he raised his arm in anger to strike his father. As he did so, his hand shriveled up, and at the same time the ground swallowed him up to his waist.

Then the people began to pray and pray, but they couldn't free him, so then they tried to dig him out. The more they dug, the farther down he went, not to mention the fact that the dirt was holding him back until he dried up from the waist down.

Then the son promised God that if He got him out, he would roam the four corners of the earth for the rest of his life, preaching the word of God and what had happened to him with his father so that sons and daughters of other parents wouldn't be mean to their parents—and would obey them. If not, they would suffer the same fate as he had.

After God opened up the earth and the son was set free, he kept his promise. He roamed the four corners of the earth until he died.

I've Been Bewitched So Many Times

You can't imagine the number of times I've been bewitched, but some of them have been really horrible. Two of them have been so awful that they've practically sent me to the grave, but the good spirits keep coming back. Whenever they see me about to drop dead, they revive me, and that's what happened to me this one time. I won't say where, but it occurred in 1950, when my lungs collected a lot of blood.

Huge globs of blood from my lungs! The doctor gave me three days to live. Three days!

I remember that it was a Tuesday and then on Wednesday I

Lala Gallegos

había dicho el dotor, y loo la médica me dijo la misma cosa que el dotor. Yo no le dije naa a la médica, y echando sangre siempre por la boca. Y bien débil es que estaba. Pesaba menos de 90 libras.

Y luego compré hierbas de polvo de esta curandera. Estaan toas regüeltas: alfarfa, cadillo, manzanilla. De todos los remedios que se usan hoy en día, pero toos regüeltos. Taa tengo las dos cajitas. Me los dio [la curandera] pa que me bebiera como té. En menos de los seis días ya yo andaba bien.

El mono de puro cabello

Éste es diún hombre que le sacaron un monito. Ése es verdá porque lo vi con mis ojos yo. No vo a dijir el lugar tampoco, pero le tenían hecho mal a este hombre, y logo vino un médico, un curandero, y le dijo que él más o menos dijía quiénes eran las personas que le tenían hecho mal.

Vino y en el mero *driveway* ahí hizo un pozo este hombre; era espirituista y sabizo. Escarbó y de ahi sacó un frasco de adentro del pozo. Era un frasco que enpaca uno chile verde, y adentro estaba el mono de puro cabello de mujer. Era cabello largo, y el mono estaba bien hecho, conforme es un mono, y loo cosido con correa. Y lo sacó y loo nos dijo que lo quemáranos. Lo quemamos y cuando ya lo quemamos era el esqueleto diún pajarito, o diún ratón. Y ése era el mal que le tenían puesto a este hombre.

Eso era lo que le estaba a él mortificando y no lo estaba mortificando malamente, solamente poco a poquito. Esto pasó como en el mes de junio y pal mes de diciembre, de ese mismo año, iba ser muerto si no se le había sacao en tiempo. Ya ni iba garrar ni resuello. Lo iban a matar. Y éstas eran tres mujeres las que lo tenían asina.

Era en el *driveway* onde parábanos la troca día por día, y noche por noche. A este hombre le hicieron el mal aquí en Villanueva, pero esta gente [su familia] vivía ajuera de Villanueva, en otro estao,

Lala Gallegos

went to a female folk healer. Then I was to die on the following day. That's what the doctor himself had told me, and then the folk healer told me the same thing. I didn't say anything to the folk healer, all the while spitting blood. And I guess I was terribly weak; I weighed less than 90 pounds.

Then I went and bought some powder herbs from this particular folk healer. The herbs were all mixed together: alfalfa, cocklebur, chamomile, all of the herbal remedies that are used nowadays, but they were all mixed together. I still have the two little boxes. The folk healer gave them to me to drink like a tea. In less than six days I was well again.

A Doll Made of Pure Hair

*T*his is the story about this man who had a witch's tiny doll inside his stomach and the folk healer took it out. That's true because I saw it with my own eyes. I'm not going to name the place either, but this man was bewitched, and then a folk practitioner, a healer, came and he told the man more or less who the evil persons were who had put on the spell.

The folk healer came and dug a small hole right in the driveway; he was a spiritualist and wise. He dug a hole and from there he took out a jar. It was a pint-size jar like one used for canning green chile, and inside the jar was a witch's doll made out of real woman's hair. The hair was long, and the doll was well-made, just as a doll should be, and then sewn with leather-type shoestrings. Then the healer took it out and told us to burn it. We burned it, and once we had finished burning it, the skeleton turned out to be that of a tiny bird, or that of a mouse. That's the evil that had been cast on this man.

That's what was torturing that man, and it wasn't tormenting him badly, just a little bit at a time. This happened on or about the month of June, and by December of that same year he would have been dead if the woven-hair doll had not been taken out in time. By that time he wouldn't have even been able to breathe. They were going to kill him. There were three women who had him suffering like that.

Lala Gallegos

y el espirituista, él vino y sacó el mal para que el hombre no sufiera más. Él mismo lo llevó pallá onde estbaba el mal.

Nojotros juimos y anduvimos onde parábanos la troca porque el curandero iba venir en la tarde a las cuatro. Esa tierra estaba tan dura como si juera puro cimente. Tuvimos que echale agua y echale agua pa que se ablandara la tierra. El enfermo escarbó primero y lego el médico escarbó al último pa sacar el mono él. Y le dijo al enfermo que no se juera andar espantando, y que rezara too lo que pudiera, porque era espantoso lo que iba a ver, la cosa que iba sacar. Y eso jue lo que sacó—un mono. Era la figura de una vieja y el cabello era negro con canas. Era un puro mono con manitas, patitas y cabeza, y delgadito. Y loo lo quemamos, pero sanó el hombre.

Lala Gallegos

It was in the driveway, where we used to park the truck day after day, night after night. This man was inflicted with the evil spell here in Villanueva, but his family lived outside Villanueva, in another state. But the spiritualist came and took out the evil spirit so that the man wouldn't suffer here anymore. He himself took him over there where the evil spirit was.

We went and checked things where we used to park the truck because the healer was going to show up at four o'clock in the afternoon. That dirt was hard as if it were solid cement. We had to pour more and more water so that the dirt softened up. The sick man dug first and then the healer dug last so that he would be the one to take out the witch's doll. And he warned the sick man not to go get scared, and for him to pray as much as he could, because what he was about to see was frightening. And that's what he dug up—a witch's doll. It was the figure of an old woman and her hair was black and gray, salt and pepper like. It was a real witch's doll with little hands, little feet, and a head, and very thin. Then we burned it, and the sick man was cured.

73

Lala Gallegos

Pedro V. Gallegos

PEDRO V. GALLEGOS

Nació: El 22 de septiembre, 1912
Villanueva, NM
Entrevista: El 9 de febrero, 1996
Villanueva, NM

Born: September 22, 1912
Villanueva, NM
Interview: February 9, 1996
Villanueva, NM

Esta muchacha bonita

*T*e iba a platicar de este hombre que se mantenía en las borregas, y le gustaba muncho la cerveza, le gustaban muncho los bailes. En una ocasión—esto me platicaba mi padre a mí—se le metió en la cabeza y en esta ocasión ensilló su caballo moro y se vino pacá [a Villanueva].

Cuando llegó a la Placita aquí, el hombre amarraba su caballo hasta que pasaba el baile y loo se golvía ir pal campo. En esta ocasión cuando llegó a la sala de baile, paí antes de ir al baile, buscó un lugar onde amarrar su caballo. Cuando llegó al lugar onde iba amarrar su caballo, se apió y ahi estaba una viejita esperándolo a él. Y le dice la viejita al muchacho,

—No te fijes. Ahi déjame el caballo. Yo lo asisto. Amárralo con tu cabrestante. Yo lo asisto. Déjamelo.

Pus aquél se jue confiao. Por qué le confió a la mujer no sé. Puede que la conociera. Cuando entró al baile, pus, anda vete había muncha gente, pero esta muchacha bonita lo buscó; lo prefirió desdiún prencipio. Pues, ya no bailó con nadien más de con ella too el baile. Zas y zas y bebe y bebe cerveza.

Al último cuando ya se acabó el baile se desapareció la bruja y isque pasó, pero ya él ya andaba a gatas. Se jue par onde estaba su caballo. Ahi estaba la viejita esperándolo otra vez, pero ya él no sabía si iba o vinía. Ya andaba muy embolao.

Pero dicía en papá que dijía el muchacho después de que ya menió la cabeza poco, que llegó al campo onde estaba él con los animales, pus se amarró el caballo y se apió. Él no sabe cómo se apió del caballo pero se apió del caballo y figuraba él quizás como que alguien lo iba detener porque iba tan mal que no alcanzaba a comprender más allá. Pues otro día en la mañana jalló su caballo desensillao, bien comido, y too bonito, y él no supo quién sería. Ésa es una de las [historias] que me platicaba en papá a mí.

Pedro V. Gallegos

This Beautiful Girl

I was going to tell you about this man who used to spend his time taking care of sheep, and he liked beer a lot, he liked dances. One time—this is what my father used to tell me—on this one occasion he saddled up his bluish-gray horse and he headed this way [to Villanueva].

When he got here to the Placita, he would tie his horse until the dance was over and then he'd return to his campsite. This one time when he got to the dance hall, before going in to dance, he looked for a place to tie his horse. When he reached the place where he was going to tie the horse, he dismounted and there was a little old lady waiting for him. And she says to him:

"Don't worry. Just leave the horse there for me. I'll take care of it. Tie it with your rope. I'll take care of it. Just leave it there for me."

Well, the man left with confidence. Why he trusted the woman I have no idea. Perhaps he knew her. When he entered the dance hall, well, there were a lot of people there, but this pretty girl was looking for him; she preferred him from the very beginning. Well, he didn't dance with anybody else all night long, just her. Dancing and dancing and drinking and drinking beer.

Toward the end when the dance was over, the witch, that is, the girl, disappeared and that was it, but he was already on all fours [drunk]. He headed for his horse. There was the little old lady waiting once again, but he no longer knew whether he was coming or going. He was already very drunk.

But my dad used to say that the boy, after shaking his head a bit, after he got to the campsite where he was camping with his animals, well, he got down and tied up his horse. He doesn't know how he got down from the horse, but get down he did and he was worried that someone would hold him up because he was in such bad shape that he couldn't understand anything. Well, the next morning he found his horse unsaddled, well fed, and groomed, but he didn't know who had done it. That's one of the stories my dad used to tell me.

77

Pedro V. Gallegos

Volaban brasas

Y luego esta otra historia de la casa que te digo, que era la casa de las brujas, aá en el corral. Eso platicaban antes de que yo comprara ese lugar, que volaban brasas diondequiera, pa la casa esa. Y iba gente a visitala [a una bruja] cuando no estaban ellas juntas o lo que juera. Dicía una mujer quisque una destas brujas tenía como un cajón con un ajuero, y en este ajuero nomás llegabas tú a la casa o a la puerta que abría, pronto iba y se sentaba en el ajuero pa que no supieran qué tenía ella ahi.

Pero en una descuidada que se dio la viejita alguien se puso abusao y jue a ver qué había ahi. Estaba llena de lagartijos y esos lagartijos isque los desollaban y con ésos hacían el polvo pa hacele mal a la gente.

Ése es ahi en la casa esa que tenemos ahi nosotros, aá bajo en el corral. Yo y tú estábanos sentaos en el cuartito que sigue, l'otra vez que estuvimos allá. Yo la teché cuando compré el lugar y puse pa poner los fierros y las sillas y todo. Y ése es lo que tenía yo de dicirte deso.

Y estaban unos rancheros. Falta que jueron borregueros hasta unos. Y llegó al instante que estaban ellos platicando, llegó uno dellos en su caballo y lo amarró adelante de la carpa. Y en lo que estaban ellos comiendo, bebiendo café, llegó una vaca, y le lambió las cabezadas del freno al caballo. Y uno dellos muy abusao, ya estaba quemao, y llegó y isque le dijo,

—Ésa no es vaca. Ésa es una bruja.

Agarró la pistola y le tronó, pero tuvo la chanza la vaca de salir juyendo y perderse, de modo que pronto se desapareció la bruja. Otro día aquí—aquí jue eso—pero el caso pasó en el campo, y aquí [en Villanueva] otro día vinieron ellos pacá y jallaron que se había muerto una viejita, con un balazo.

Pus, lo que dijía la gente. Yo no creo en nada deso, porque yo anduve muncho, muncho anduve a caballo a horas y deshoras de la noche sin *not even* brasas.

Pedro V. Gallegos

Sparks Flew All Over the Place

And then there's this other story about this house where witches lived, right there in the corral that I mentioned to you. That's what people used to talk about, that sparks flew all over the place, in the direction of that house. That was before I bought the place. And people would go visit this one witch when the other witches were not together. This lady used to say that one of these witches had a wooden box with a hole, and as soon as you got to her house or the door, she would quickly open it [raise it like a lid] and sit on the hole so people wouldn't know what she had in it.

But one time when the little old lady, the witch, got careless, someone got brave and daring and went to see what was in the hole. It was full of lizards, and I understand that she would skin those lizards, so goes the story, and that's what she used to make powder from to bewitch people with.

That happened there in that home that we have there, down the road, inside the corral. You and I were sitting in the small room next to it the last time we were over there. I roofed it when I bought the place and I fixed it to store my tools and saddles and everything. And that's what I had to tell you about that house.

Then there were also these ranchers. Perhaps some of them were even sheepherders. A particular moment came when they were all talking, whereupon another one of the ranchers arrived on his horse and tied it up in front of the tent. And while they were eating and drinking coffee, a cow showed up, and it licked the forehead part of the horse's bridle. And one of them in a very sarcastic voice, he was already very burned out [experienced], came up to them and said:

"That's not a cow, that's a witch."

He grabbed his pistol and shot at it, but the cow was lucky enough to take off running and get lost, so that the witch quickly disappeared. The next day—the actual incident occurred in the countryside—and the next day the ranchers came here to Villanueva and found out that a little old lady had died from a bullet wound.

Well, that's what people used to say. I don't believe any of that, because I traveled a lot on horseback at all hours of the night without ever seeing any sparks.

Pedro V. Gallegos

Regino Gallegos

REGINO GALLEGOS

Nació: El 23 de mayo, 1924
Villanueva, NM
Entrevista: El 22 de agosto, 1989
Villanueva, NM

Born: May 23, 1924
Villanueva, NM
Interview: August 22, 1989
Villanueva, NM

Relatos cortitos

Iban dos en el burro y el que iba atrás era el güeno y el que iba adelante era el diablo. Y loo le dijo el que iba atrás al que iba adelante,

—¡Pícale la cruz!

Cuando le picó la cruz al burro, el de adelante se despareció. Era la cosa mala.

～ ～ ～

Y loo un muchacho que iba pal Cerrito a ver a la novia. Ése oyó llorar una mujer, en una ventana, y dice que él no figuraba a esas horas que hubiera una mujer. Y no más golvió a ver novias de noche. Tenía que velas de día.

～ ～ ～

Era en papá el que vido esto. Vinían él y otros de las Salinas. Antonces usaban carros de güeyes, no bestias. Y en tal día, como el tercer día antes del viaje, había pisao uno de los güeyes el nido de una culebra. Tres días después se acordó en papá onde había sido esto. Y loo lo siguió la churrionela por tres días y se jue derecho al mismo güey que había pisao el nido. Aá se comenzó azotalo la culebra al güey. Antonces en papá le pegó a la culebra con la borreguera que llevaba puesta. Él se acordó del troncón y tiró la leva arriba. Tuvo la oportunidá de ponela en un troncón, y de ahi comenzó la culebra azotala [la borreguera] hasta que se mató sola.

Regino Gallegos

Short Little Narratives

There were two guys on a donkey and the one riding in back was the good guy and the one in front [in the saddle] was the devil. Then the one riding in back said to the one in front:

"Spur it in the crotch!"

When he spurred the donkey's crotch, the one riding in front disappeared. It was an evil spirit.

₰ ₰ ₰

Then there was this boy who was on his way to El Cerrito to visit his girlfriend. He heard a woman cry from a window, and he says that he couldn't imagine why a woman would be there at that hour. That was the end of seeing girlfriends at night. He decided to see them during the day.

₰ ₰ ₰

My father is the one who saw this snake. He and some others were on their way back from Salinas. At that time they used oxen to pull the wagons, not horses. And one day, about three days before the trip, one of the oxen had stepped on a snake's nest. Three days later my father remembered where this had happened. Then the bullwhip snake followed him for three days and it went straight to the ox that had stepped on the nest. That's when the bullwhip snake starting whipping the ox. Then my father beat it with the sheepskin jacket that he had on. He remembered a tree trunk and tossed his jacket on top of it. My father was lucky to put the jacket on the tree trunk and from then on the snake whipped the sheepskin jacket until it killed itself.

Regino Gallegos

Valerio García

VALERIO GARCÍA

Nació: El 12 de mayo, 1923
San José, NM
Entrevista: El 24 de agosto, 1989
Ribera, NM

Born: May 12, 1923
San José, NM
Interview: August 24, 1989
Ribera, NM

Él nomás platicaba con su gato

El cuento que dicían de en aquellos tiempos [era] cuando los animales hablaban. Había es que cerca de un reinado un muchacho llamado Juan. Tenía un gato. Y él nomás platicaba con su gato porque nadien había cerca más dél. Ahí cerquías dionde él vivía en una chocita chica había unos ladrones. Estos ladrones robaban muncho en dondequiera. Tenían munchos ganaos: vacas, borregas, caballos. De todo tenían. Muncha plata.

Pues una vez es que le dice el gato,

—Hermano Juan, ¿por qué no se casa con la hija del rey? En el reinado publicaron de que ya la hija tiene edá pa casarse—.

Le dijo Juan,

—¡Pero qué me voy a casar yo! No tengo ni nada—.

—Pero sí—le dijo el gato. —Tenemos a nuestros amigos, los ladrones estos.

Cada vez que ellos salían le encargaban a Juan las casas. Le dijo,

—Nomás haz lo que yo te diga y te casas con la hija del rey.

Por fin Juan aceptó y el gato se jue al reinado y pidió la mano de la hija del rey al rey. Le dijo el rey,

—Güeno, pus, ¿qué tiene Juan?

—Tiene de todo. Tiene lo que tú tienes o más.

Le dijo el rey,

—Bien. Ve allá y dile a Juan que venga."

Pues Juan jue. Se casaron. Hicieron un fiestín de dos semanas. De todo tenían. Pos cabándose ya la fiesta, que ya tenían que irse, es que le dice Juan al gatito,

—¿Ora qué vamos hacer? Ora mi suegro quiere ir a conocer. Y no tengo nada.

Y dijo el gato,

—No te preocupes. Yo voy contigo. Tú haz lo que yo te diga y nada más.

Pues salió el rey con toda su gente, con trompetas y todo pa llegar al rancho de Juan. Entraron en los primeros ranchos y dice el rey,

—¡Pero qué ganao tan grande se mira aquí!

—Es de mi hermano Juan—dice el gato.

Valerio García

He Only Talked to His Cat

*T*his is the story of yesteryear when animals used to talk. The story concerns a certain Juan who lived close to a kingdom. He had a cat. And he would only talk to his cat because there was nobody else around but his cat. Close to where he lived in a little shack were several thieves. These thieves robbed everywhere they went. They had a lot of livestock: cattle, sheep, and horses. They had everything. Lots of money.

Well, one time the cat said to him: "Brother Juan, why don't you marry the king's daughter? They have made it public throughout the kingdom that the daughter is already old enough to get married."

Juan said to the cat: "But how can I marry her? I don't own anything."

"But you do," said the cat. "We have our friends, these thieves of ours." Every time they went away they left Juan in charge of their homes. Said the cat: "All you have to do is do as I say and you'll be able to marry the king's daughter."

Finally Juan accepted the idea and the cat left for the kingdom and asked the king for his daughter's hand in marriage. The king said to him, "Very well, but what does Juan own?"

"He has everything you have or perhaps even more."

Said the king: "Very well. Go back and tell Juan to come here." Well, Juan went as per the king's wishes.

The king's daughter and Juan got married. They held a huge celebration that lasted for two weeks. They had everything, all kinds of food. Well, when the celebration was about to end, when everyone was about to leave, Juan said to the little cat, "Now what are we going to do? My father-in-law now wants to go see my place. I don't have anything."

And he responded, "Don't worry. I'll go with you. You do as I say and nothing more."

Well, the king took off with all of his people, accompanied by trumpets and all, heading to Juan's ranch. They got to the first ranches and the king said, "What a large herd of cattle can be seen here!"

"It belongs to my brother Juan," said the cat.

Valerio García

Y loo pasaron más allá y es que dijo el rey,

—¡Cuánta borrega! ¡Miles!

—Son de mi hermano Juan—pus es que dice el gato.

Caminaron más allá y llegó una caballada grandísima.

—¡Cuánto caballo!

—Son de mi hermano Juan—dice el gato.

Pus el gato se les despareció. Y corrió adelante y llegó a case de los vecinos, los ladrones, y les dijo él,

—Manitos. ¡Retírense! Pronto viene el rey con toa su gente.

Pos aquéllos oyeron las trompetas y el gentío que iba. Pronto ensillaron los caballos y les dijo uno de ellos,

—¡Vámonos! Ahi le encargamos a Juan todo hasta que se vaya el rey.

—Está bien—les dijo el gato.

—Ahi están las llaves—dijo un ladrón.

Pues el gato agarró las llaves y cuando llegó el rey, lo recibió el gato y dijo,

—Lleguen. Pasen por acá.

Es que estaban las casas grandísimas.

—Quiero enseñales señor rey lo que tiene mi hermano Juan aquí.

Abrió el primer cuarto y estaba que se salían las monedas. Eran puros nicles y cerró pronto las puertas. Abrió lotro y dijo,

—Mire acá. Allá daimes—y lo cerró.

Abrió lotro. Puras pesetas. Abrió el otro y eran *half dollars* y es que le dijo el rey,

—¿Y aquel cuarto grande?

—No, ahí tenemos el oro.

Y loo es que dice el rey,

—¡Vámonos! Este hombre está más rico que yo, que soy el rey.

Se golvió el rey contoy sus gentes pal reinado, y Juan y su mujer se quedaron ahí en la choza que tenían. Ella taavía no comprendía si tenían riqueza o no tenían pero vivían ahí nomás con su estufa de leña y su gato. Pus una mañana el gato se quedó acostao atrás de la estufa y se hizo el muerto. Le dice ella a su marido,

—Juanito. El gatito está muerto—.

Le dice Juan,

—Agárralo de la cola y tíralo aá juera.

Antonces se levanta el gato y dice,

—¡Ah hermano Juan! ¡Qué bien me paga por todo lo que hice por usté!

Valerio García

Then they went on up a ways and the king said, "So many sheep! Thousands!"

"They belong to my brother Juan," said the cat.

They walked a ways and a large herd of horses showed up. "So many horses!"

"They belong to my brother Juan," said the cat.

Well, the cat disappeared on them. He ran on up ahead and he arrived at the neighbors' home, that of the thieves, and he said, "My dear brothers. Scoot! The king will be here soon with all of his people."

About that time the thieves heard the trumpets and the large group of people that was coming. Quickly they saddled up their horses and one of the thieves said to the rest of them: "Let's go! We'll leave everything in Juan's hands until the king departs."

"That's fine!" said the cat.

"There are the keys," said one of the thieves.

Well, the cat grabbed the keys and when the king arrived, the cat greeted him and said, "Come in. This way." The homes, according to people, were huge. "I want to show you, your majesty, what my brother Juan owns here." He opened the first room and it was bulging with coins. They were all nickels, and he closed the doors quickly. He opened the next room and said, "Take a look there. Those are dimes," and he closed the doors.

He opened the next room. It was nothing but *pesetas* [Spanish coins]. He opened the next room and there were half-dollars, and about that time the king said to the cat, "And what about that huge room?"

"Why no," he said, "That's where we have the gold."

Then the king said, "Let's go! This man [Juan] is richer than I, the king."

The king then returned to his kingdom with all of his entourage, and Juan and his wife stayed back in the shack that they had. She still didn't understand whether she and her husband had any wealth or not, but there they lived next to their wood stove and their cat. One morning, the cat was resting behind the stove pretending to be dead, and she said to him, "My dear Juan. The cat is dead."

Said Juan, "Grab it by the tail and toss it outside."

About that time the cat got up and said, "Oh, brother Juan! What a way to pay me for everything that I did for you."

Valerio García

Las dos eran brujas

*H*abía en un lugar una mujer y tenía una hija muy hermosa. La señora era bruja, pero en el pueblo no sabían que la mujer era bruja, y estaba enseñando a su hija también a bruja. Pus llega por ese pueblo un joven, muy bien parecido, y la muchacha loo se enamoró de él, y le dijo a la mamá y a la mamá le gustó. Se casó con la muchacha.

Pus a los cuantos días vio él que en las noches se desparecían la suegra y su esposa. No sabía par ónde se iban y se levantaba y las puertas cerradas. Ya empezó a quedarse despierto y vio que se levantaban. En una repesita que tenían en un rincón, tenían una botellita con un pomito. Éstas se levantaban y agarraban de aquel pomo y se untaban en todas las coyonturas y salían por la bujero de la llave, porque él tenía las llaves pa que no salieran pero salían por la bujero de la llave.

Antonces hizo él la misma: se untó de aquel pomito. También salió atrás de ella y las halló en el camposanto. Habían sacado el cuerpo de un muerto y estaban comiendo carne cuando él llegó. Pus la vieja se endemonió muncho cuando vio que las había agarrao en el caso y lo volvió un perro.

Le echó pedradas y el pobre perro pus corrió y sale la perrada del pueblo atrás dél—todos los perros lo andaban mordiendo porque era un perro estraño. Pus ya él en la madrugada se acurrucó en la puerta de un panadero. Ya el panadero estaba ahí haciendo su pan cuando vio que la perrada ya se comía aquel perro. Abrió la puerta y lo metió pa dentro. Estaba muy mal herido, muy lastimao. Y empezó a curarlo; lo tenía aá dentro. No lo dejaba salir porque había muncha perrada.

A los cuantos días que ya descansó vio que aquel perro entendía todo lo que él le decía y empezó a hacelo mandaditos y a mandale más y aquel animal todo sabía. Antonces vio que este perro llegó hasta el punto que sabía dar cambio. Sabía las clases del pan. Publicó el panadero en los papeles que tenía un asistente que era su perro y que el perro podía aprender a las gentes a que compraran el pan de sus gustos y el mismo perro les daba el cambio. Pos empezó a venir la gente de a millares por ver aquel perro. Le pidía pan del que

Valerio García

The Two Were Witches

There was a woman in this particular place and she had a very beautiful daughter. The woman was a witch, but in the village the people didn't know that she was a witch. She was also teaching her daughter how to be a witch. Well, a young man, very handsome, happened by that village, and the girl quickly fell in love with him. She told her mom about it and her mother liked the idea. He married the girl.

Well, after a few days he noticed that his mother-in-law and his wife would disappear at night. He didn't know where they went, but he would get up and find the doors locked. He started staying awake at night. He saw that they would get up. In a small mantle in a corner they kept a tiny bottle with a little bit of scent. The ladies would get up, grab some of that scent, put it all over their joints, and then exit through the keyhole, because he had kept the keys so they couldn't go out. But they'd do so just the same, through the keyhole.

Then he did the same thing: He rubbed himself with some of that scent. He also left right behind them and found them at the cemetery. They had dug up the body of a dead person and were eating flesh when he arrived. Well, the old lady became furious when she realized that he had caught them in the act and she turned him into a dog.

She tossed rocks at him, and when the poor dog ran, a pack of dogs chased after him—all of the dogs were biting him because he was a stranger to them. Well, when morning came he huddled at the door of a baker. The baker was already baking his bread when he saw that the pack was about to put an end to the dog. He opened the door and let him inside. The dog was injured quite a bit, hurt very badly. And he started to nurse his wounds; he kept him inside. He wouldn't let him go outside because there were too many dogs.

A few days later when the dog was already well, the baker noticed that the dog understood everything he said to him, and so he started to ask him to run little errands and more errands. That animal knew how to do everything. He saw that the dog even got to the point where he knew how to make change. He could tell the different kinds of bread. The baker published in the newspapers that

Valerio García

estaba más alto y subía el perro por la escalera y se los bajaba. Le ponían el dinero allí y les daba el cambio. Pus muy azorada toa la gente de ver aquel animal tan entendido.

En esto se dio cuenta uno que era arbolario. El arbolario vino, compró pan y se esperó a que hubiera poca gente y loo le dice,

—¡Oyes! Tú no eres un perro. Eres un ser humano que te volvieron perro, pero yo soy arbolario—le dijo—y yo te vuelvo a tu naturalez. Esta noche a las doce te espero en tal lugar.

Pos sí, a las doce ahi llegó el perro. Pronto lo volvió la persona que era. Le dijo,

—Quiero que a mi esposa me la vuelva una potranca.

—Está bien. Ahora en la mañana voy a ir y va ser una potranca.

Pus en la mañana fue. Se puso unas buenas espuelas bastante puntiagudas y la montó y empezó a correla por todo el pueblo, clavándole las espuelas por todas partes hasta que le corría la sangre. La vieja la vio y de lo que vido que estaba haciendo con la hija se murió de una ataque de corazón. Aquél le dio a la potranca hasta que cayó muerta. De la potranca que estaba muerta se volvió la persona que era. Antonces en el pueblo se dieron cuenta de que las dos, la vieja y la hija, eran brujas.

92

Valerio García

he had an assistant who was a dog and that the dog could teach people how to purchase the bread of their choice and that the dog himself would give them back change. Well, people started to go by the thousands just to see that dog. Someone would ask him for bread that was higher up and the dog would climb up the ladder and then he would climb down. People would put down the money and the dog would give them back change. All of the people were very surprised to see such a well-behaved and intelligent animal.

Then an herbalist took notice of the dog. The herbalist came, bought bread, waited until there were few people around and then said to him:

"Hey there! You're not a dog. You're a human being who was turned into a dog. But I'm an herbalist," he said to him, "and I'll turn you back to your natural state. Tonight at twelve o'clock I'll wait for you at such-and-such a place."

So at twelve o'clock the dog was there. Quickly the herbalist turned him into the person that he was before. He said to the herbalist:

"I want you to turn my wife into a young filly."

"Very well. This very morning I'm going to go see her and she'll become a young filly."

Well, morning came and he went. The man put on a pair of very sharp spurs and he got on the filly and he started to run her all over the village, digging his spurs here and there until blood was running. The old lady saw what he was doing to her daughter and died from a heart attack. That man ran that filly until she dropped dead. The dead filly turned into the person that she was before. Then the people in the village came to realize that the old lady and the daughter were two witches.

Valerio García

La Llorona

Contaban que todas mis gentes por aquí oían la Llorona. Yo de mi parte nunca, ni lo creí. Hubo un tiempo [que leí] el libro de la Llorona, pa desengañarme qué era la Llorona, de dónde venía, o por qué las gentes dicían que oían la Llorona.

En este libro dice que en la época como del siglo trece mataban a las personas que dicían que eran brujas. Y a esta mujer la ataron a un poste para quemarla viva porque dicían que era una bruja. Esto procedió de España. Cuando la ataron para quemarla, ya le digo que quemaron una persona inocente que no era bruja. Y si quemaban una persona inocente, que no era bruja, la iban a oyer llorar, y sus descendientes de las personas que la quemaran, la deberían llorar por siglos. Esa noche cuando la quemaron, tenían unos parientes los que la quemaron, veinte millas de lejos. De allá la oyeron llorar.

Y dese tiempo hasta orita, reclama la gente, la han oído llorar, por todas partes del mundo que los españoles conquistaron en un tiempo. De maneras que hay gentes desparramadas, descendientes de aquellas personas que quemaron a esta señora que, hasta orita, la oyen llorar.

Yo no creo. No soy descendiente porque no la he oido.

Valerio García

The Wailing Woman

*P*eople were accustomed to saying that all of my people around here used to hear the Wailing Woman. As for me, I never heard her, nor did I believe in it. One time I did read a book about the Wailing Woman, just so I could find out for myself what the Wailing Woman was all about, where she came from, or why people claimed that they could hear the Wailing Woman.

In this book it says that during the thirteenth century they used to kill the persons who were supposedly witches. And this one particular woman, they tied her to a post so as to burn her alive because people claimed she was a witch. All of this came from Spain. When they tied her to the post to burn her, as I understand it, they burned an innocent person who was not a witch. And if they burned an innocent woman, those who burned her, as well as their descendants, were going to hear her cry for centuries to come. On the night that they burned her, some of their relatives, 20 miles away, heard her cry.

And from that time onward, until right this very moment, they've heard her wail—so say the people—throughout all parts of the world that the Spaniards conquered. So there's people scattered all over the globe who are descendants of those persons who burned this woman, who up until today can hear her wail.

I don't believe it. I guess I'm not a descendant of hers because I haven't heard her.

Valerio García

Se acabó la Llorona

Bueno, una llorona dijieron que había ahi en San José, pero no era tal cosa. Munchas gentes dicían que la habían visto, vistida de blanco. Ahi estaba arribita de San José. Todas las tardes la vían unas gentes y otras.

Yo le pedí permiso a mi papá pa ir con el rifle a matar la Llorona. Mi papá dijo que estaba loco, que no había tal cosa. Mi papá tampoco no creía en lloronas, ni en bultos, ni en nada deso. En papá dicía que todo lo que mirabas en el día estaba en la noche, nomás en la noche no se miraba tan bien.

Y es verdá. Así es la cosa. Porque usté ve que si munchas gentes meten miedo con un difunto, ya uno que se muere no se levanta. Si está muerto, no se va levantar. Si está vivo sí, pero un muerto no se levanta, y menos enterrao.

De todos modos, es que estaba una llorona, una bruja ahi. Estaba yo mediano, como de diez y seis años, una cosa así. Le pedí el permiso a mi papá de ir con un rifle a buscala y dijo mi papá,

—¿Cuál rifle?

No tenía, pero un pariente nuestro tenía un 30–30 y jui a pedile el rifle. Dijo,

—Pos sí. ¿Qué vas a hacer?

—A ver si jallo la Llorona esa.

Él estaba como mi papá. Dijo,

—No hay tal cosa, pero yo te empresto el rifle. Únicamente que cartuchos no tengo. ¿Y quién tendrá?—dijo—. —Puede que el vecino Pablo tenga. Él también tiene un 30–30.

Jui a case de don Pablo a que me prestara cartuchos. Jui allí y me dijo,

—Pos, ¿y sabe tu papá?

Le dije,

—Pos mi papá me da el permiso porque mi papá no cree que hay Llorona.

—Ni yo tampoco—dijo—. No hay, pero vamos a ver a tu papá. Vino y le dijo a mi papá,

—¡Mira! ¿Que es verdá que lo dejas ir?

—Sí—le dijo en papá—. Aá que se esté. Al cabo no va hallar

Valerio García

That Was the End of the Wailing Woman

O kay, people used to say that there was a wailing woman there in San José, but there was no such thing. Lots of people would say that they had seen her, dressed in white. There she'd be, right on up by San José. All kinds of people would see her every evening.

I asked my dad for permission to go with the rifle to kill the Wailing Woman. My dad said that I was crazy, that there was no such thing. He didn't believe in wailing women either, nor in ghosts, nor in anything like that. My dad used to say that everything you saw during the day you'd see at night, except that at night you couldn't see it very well.

And it's true. That's the way things are. Because you can see that if lots of people try to scare you with a dead person, once a person dies it doesn't get up. If it's dead, it can't get up. If the person is alive, yes, but a dead person, no, least of all if it's buried.

Anyway, they say that there used to be a wailing woman, a witch around there; that's what people said. I was young, about 16 years old, something like that. I asked my dad for permission to go with the rifle to look for her and he said: 97

"What rifle?"

He didn't have one, but a relative of ours had a 30–30, and I went and asked him for it. He said:

"Why yes. What are you going to do?"

"I'm going to see if I can find the Wailing Woman."

His reaction was like that of my father. He said:

"There's no such thing, but I'll lend it to you. The only thing is that I don't have any shells. And who knows who's got any? Perhaps my neighbor Pablo has some. He's got a 30–30."

I went to Don Pablo's house so he could lend me some shells. I went there and he said to me, "Well, does your father know about this?"

I said to him, "My father has given me permission because he doesn't believe that the Wailing Woman exists."

"Neither do I," he said. "There is no such thing, but let's go see your father."

He went and he said to my father:

Valerio García

nada. Pus no hay tal cosa.

Ya cuando vine patrás con el permiso, a que don Pablo me diera los cartuchos, jui por el rifle, y don Pablo agarró unos cartuchos y se jue conmigo. Yo llevaba el rifle y él los cartuchos. ¡Qué cosa tan bien! ¿Y de qué me sirvía? Pus llegamos allá a una de las arboleras y pus era en el mes de agosto. Había munchas verduras y árboles y todo. Nos sentamos abajo de un árbol y antonces me dio él un cartucho y se lo puse al rifle, a esperar que saliera aquella llorona. No. No salía nada. Pos sale una pobre señora allá con un vestido blanco y levanté el rifle pa tumbala. Nomás que don Pablo me levantó el rifle parriba y el tiro se jue parriba y dijo,

—¿Que estás loco?

Pus era mujer. Naturalmente le iba tirar un balazo. La culpa jue della que andaba vistida de blanco. Asina dicían que se vistía la Llorona.

Don Pablo me quitó el rifle y se jue a hablar con ella. De allá pacá vino regañándome, que vámonos pa la casa y dijo,

—¡Tú estás loco hombre!

Y le iba a tirar. Pus le dije yo que era la Llorona. No, pus no era. Pobre persona. Quién sabe quién sería porque don Pablo nunca dijo. Pero se acabó la Llorona.

La gente reclamaba de que la mujer recogía verduras y eso de allí de las labores en las tardes. Y si miraba a alguien le pegaba un llorido y salía corriendo y dicían que aá andaba la Llorona. El día que llegaban al pueblo avisar, ya ella no estaba. No estaba pa nada.

Son cosas del mundo y nada más. Yo no creo que haiga ni brujas, ni diablos, ni nada deso. Si el diablo está, está como está nuestro Dios—onde no lo vemos. Porque a Dios no lo vemos, pero sabemos que existe. Así es el diablo. Si cuando váyanos a ver a Dios, no nos recibe, allá nos va despachar con el diablo. Él tiene su lugar del diablo. Está muy separado del de Dios.

Valerio García

"Look! Is it true that you gave him permission to go?"

"Yes," said my dad. "Let him go. He's not going to find anything anyway, because there's no such thing."

By the time I got back with permission, I went after the rifle so Don Pablo would give me the bullets, and he grabbed a few bullets and took off with me. I was carrying the rifle and he the ammunition. What a nice state of affairs! What good did it do me? Well, we got to one of those orchards; it was during the month of August. There were lots of vegetables and trees and everything. We sat down underneath a tree and then he gave me a bullet and I loaded it, waiting for that wailing woman to come out. But no one came out. Then a poor woman comes out dressed in white, and I raised the rifle to shoot her down. The only thing is that he [Don Pablo] grabbed the rifle and raised it upwards and the bullet took off into the sky and he said:

"Are you crazy?"

Well, it was a woman. Naturally I was going to shoot at her. It was the woman's fault for being dressed in white. That's the way people said the Wailing Woman dressed.

Don Pablo took the rifle away from me and went to talk to her.
On the way back he kept scolding me and saying that we should go home: "Man, you're crazy!"

And I was going to shoot at her. I thought to myself that she was the Wailing Woman. No, she wasn't. Poor woman. Who knows who she was? Don Pablo never told me. But that was the end of the Wailing Woman.

People used to say that the woman would gather vegetables and that sort of thing from the fields in the evenings. And if she saw someone she would let out a holler at them and they'd take off running, so people used to say that the Wailing Woman was around. By the time people in the village were told, she was no longer around.

There's things that happen in this world and that's it. I don't believe there's any witches, or the devil, or anything like that. If the devil exists, it exists just like God—where we can't see it. Because we don't see God, but we know that He exists. That's the way the devil is. If we go see God, and He doesn't receive us, He's going to send us to visit the devil. He knows the devil's place. It's quite separate from God's.

Valerio García

Se había agarrao con el diablo

Decían que ahí en el *pool* de San José se juntaban las gentes. Y creo que un amigo de mi tío Ramón llegó y les dijo que nomás en cuanto se había acabao de dar un agarrón con el diablo. Deste lao de San José había una milpa algo grande y dijo que él los traía y les probaba que él se había agarrao con el diablo. Pos estaba la gente que no lo creía, ni que no lo creía.

Otro día vinieron. Llegaron al lugar onde él dijo que había luchao con este diablo, en medio de la milpa. Ya hallaron la milpa tumbada por todas partes y las juellas de aquel hombre y las de como una vaca, porque él es que cayó allá todo rasguñao y todo eso. Eso es lo que platicaron ahí las gentes, que andaba el diablo suelto.

Otra vez dicieron que es que vinía, qué, no sé. A mi papá le contaron que por qué él no iba con ellos. Pal rumbo del *pool* les salió corriendo un marrano, a dales trompazos a ellos y salieron corriendo todos. Se metieron al *pool* pero es que el marrano toavía quebró las puertas del *pool*, pero la gente se arrevisó y nadien jue a matalo, ni lo siguieron.

Si yo hubiera estao yo lo hubiera seguido a ver si era marrano de veras, o un marrano endiablao o lo que juera. Yo tengo que ver y ver y crer como Santo Tomás. Si miro la cosa la creo y si no la miro ahi, no.

Valerio García

He Had Tangled with the Devil

Word has it that there in the San José pool hall is where many people would get together. And I believe it was there that a friend of my uncle Ramón supposedly arrived who said that he had just had a run-in with the devil. This side of San José there was a cornfield, quite large, and he said that he would take them and show them where he had tangled with the devil. Well, people were in no mood to believe him. They didn't believe him; they simply didn't.

Next day they went to the site. They got to the place where he said he had wrestled with the devil, in the middle of the cornfield. Sure enough, they found the cornfield trampled all over, the man's tracks and those resembling a cow. He had popped in where the people were, all scratched up and that sort of thing. That's what those people said, that the devil was on the loose.

Another time they said that something was headed their way, I don't know what. They asked my father why didn't he go with them. On the way to the pool hall a pig ran out in front of them and smacked them with its snout, and they all took off running. I understand the pig broke down the pool hall doors, but the people got really scared and no one dared go after it to shoot it.

If I had been there, I would have followed it to see if it was really a pig, or a pig that had been possessed by the devil, or whatever it was. I have to see to believe, like Saint Thomas [Aquinas]. If I see the thing, I believe it, and if I don't see it, I don't believe it.

Valerio García

Vi como bultos

Cuando yo tenía quince años, que trabajaba arriba de la Mesa, salía ya en la mañana en el caballo. Empezó a llover, ¡bárbaramente! Al llegar a la orilla de la Mesa, oía yo que estaban cantando alabaos en mi pueblo, en San José.

Al pasar de allí de la Mesa, como estaba joven, sentía temor, naturalmente, pero vinía en mi caballo. Cuando de repente el caballo pegó una juila y le caminé un poco. Vi patrás y vi que estaba como una persona con un sombrero blanco o algo así. Pos por fin devolví el caballo a ver qué era aquella cosa. Era un árbol que lo había tumbado recién y estaba muy blanco ahí abajo de la lluvia y tenía un brazo de un lao. Quedaba levantao del otro lao para bajo. Parecía bien una persona, pero me di cuenta que era únicamente un árbol. [Creí que era] pus un hombre. Un hombre. ¡El miedo!

En otra vez, viniendo de Ribera a San José, como las once de la noche, vi en frente de mí como bultos, que se movían y loo se quedaban paraos y loo parecía que se levantaban y se bajaban. Y me empezó a entrar miedo y me daban ganas de volverme, pero pensé y dije,

—Si voy a case mi hermana y le digo que vi un bulto me van a decir que qué cobarde. ¿A qué le tenía miedo?

Me quedé esperando hasta que vi que se acercaba más y más y no tenía figura ni de vaca ni de caballo.

—¿Pus qué será esto?

Cuando ya vinía demasiao cerca, como a unos quince pies, empecé a buscar piedras a los laos pero no encontré. En eso llegó, me pegó en el cuerpo, y era un bonche de cizañas, una pila de cizañas que las traía el aigre. Como estaba oscuro se miraba el bulto moverse patrás y pa delante, parriba y pa bajo, y no eran más de cizañas.

Si había corrido patrás y cuento deso, habían dicho,

—No, pus, ahi anda algo, bulto o anda algo.

Y no eran más de las cizañas. No hay mejor que ir a ver, desengañarse pa que no le platiquen los que le platican a uno, como de las brujas.

Valerio García

I Saw What Looked Like Ghosts

When I was 15 years old, and working on top of the Mesa, I used to leave in the morning on horseback. It started to rain, furiously! As I got to the edge of the Mesa, I heard someone singing hymns of praise in my village, in San José.

As I went past the Mesa, because I was young, I got scared, naturally, but I was on my horse. All of a sudden the horse gave a jerk and I spurred him on up a ways. I looked back and I saw something resembling a person with a white hat or something like that. Well, finally I turned the horse around to see what that thing was. It was a tree that had recently been knocked down and was very shiny there where it was on the ground because of the rain, and a branch was to one side. It looked just like a person, but I noticed that it was only a tree. I naturally thought that it was a man. A man. What fear will do to you!

On another occasion, coming from Ribera to San José, about eleven o'clock at night, I saw in front of me what looked like ghosts—they moved one moment and then stood still and then they looked like they went up and down. And I started to get scared and I felt like turning back, but I thought for a moment and said to myself, "If I go to my sister's house and tell her that I saw a ghost, they're going to say, 'What a coward! What were you scared of?'"

I stood still, waiting until I saw that it got closer and closer; it didn't resemble either a cow or a horse. "I wonder what this is," I thought to myself. When I got really close, about 15 feet away, I started looking for rocks on either side of me but I didn't find any. About that time, it hit my body, and it was a bunch of tumbleweeds, a bunch of tumbleweeds that the wind was carrying. Since it was dark you could see the ghostlike figure move backward and forward, up and down, and all it was, was tumbleweeds.

If I had run home and told them about that, they would have said, "No, well maybe there is something, a ghost or something." And all it was, was tumbleweeds. The best thing one can do is go see, find out for yourself, so that those who like to tell you about things like witches, won't.

Valerio García

Emelinda Gonzales

EMELINDA GONZALES

Nació: El 8 de octubre, 1923
Villanueva, NM
Entrevista: El 5 de septiembre, 1989
Villanueva, NM

Born: October 8, 1923
Villanueva, NM
Interview: September 5, 1989
Villanueva, NM

Vieron un arbolario

Yo tenía un tío que era muy querido mío, y se estuvo muncho tiempo en la casa de mi mamá. Era viudo. Él quedó viudo por razón que dijían que su esposa era a la que le habían hecho mal. A ella isque le habían hecho mal. Isque ella era una mujer que tenía una voz muy bonita, que cantaba muy bonito, y cuando le hicieron este mal, ya no podía cantar ella. Se hizo como ronca. Pero en la noche dicía en papá que de las doce pa delante, que la oían cantar a ella unas cantandas, su voz, y bien bonita, y loo que es que dicía ella,

—Ora sí, por favor, déjenme descansar—como hablándole a alguien. Dicía ella,

—Déjenme descansar.

Vieron un arbolario, un curandero, y este hombre les dijo que pusieran bien atención lo que llegara afuera en la noche cuando él estaba curándola. Dicía en papá que se pusieron él y otro mi tío este, era cuñao de la mujer que estaba enferma, y se pusieron aá fuera a esperar y a estudiar y a ver qué llegaba.

Por varias noches, no llegaba nada, pero siempre que siguía la misma cosa, con que esta pobre a tales horas tenía que cantar, quizás. La demás de la noche y lo demás del día, estaba muy mala y no podía. Asegún vían ellos los que estaban mirándola, que quizás bailaban los que la estaban escuchando, porque les dicía ella,

—Déjenme descansar. Orita bailan.

En algunas palabras en veces les dicía,

—Orita siguen bailando.

Y dijía en papá que al fin una noche mientras estaban como esperando y cuidando y too, había llegao un tecolote o alguna cosa asina, un ave, y le habían tirao un balazo con la pistola. Y bien se les hacía que le habían dao, pero que otro día que la jueron a buscar no estaba. No estaba nada.

Siempre que la mujer no se pudo curar por acaso de que seguro no pescaron la persona que estaba haciendo el mal.

Emelinda Gonzales

They Consulted An Herbalist

I had an uncle who was very dear to me, and he stayed a long time at my mom's home. He was a widower. He was left a widower because, according to what people said, someone had cast an evil spell on his wife. Rumor has it that somebody had bewitched her. She was a woman who supposedly had a beautiful voice, who sang very beautifully, but once she was bewitched, she could no longer sing. Her voice became sort of hoarse. But my dad said that from midnight onward she could be heard singing songs, her voice quite beautiful, and then, once finished, she would say, "Okay now, please, let me rest," as if talking to someone. She would say, "Let me rest."

They consulted an herbalist, a folk healer, and this man told them to pay close attention to see what made an appearance outside at night, while he was attending to her. My dad said that he and another man, an uncle of mine who was a brother-in-law of the woman who was ill, went outside to wait and to study the situation and see who arrived.

For several nights, nothing made an appearance, but always the same thing happened, that is, this poor woman at certain hours sang beautifully. The rest of the night, and the rest of the day, she was very ill and couldn't sing. It seemed to those who were watching over her that perhaps some people who were listening to her were also dancing, because she'd say to them:

"Let me rest. You can dance in a little while."

Sometimes she'd say to those who were listening, "You can continue dancing in a little while."

And Dad said that finally one night while they were waiting and watching, an owl or something like that appeared, a bird perhaps, and they shot at it with a pistol. And they were absolutely sure that they had hit it, but next day when they went to look, it wasn't there. There was nothing there.

In any case, the woman was never able to be cured because they didn't catch the person who was inflicting evil on her.

Emelinda Gonzales

Lloró un coyote

Dijía mi mamá tamién que una vez una vecina de ellas, una tal mujer que vivía por acá cerca, El Guache. Estaban ella y mi hermana Adelaida planchando en la noche, porque antes planchaban con las planchas de esas de [estufa]. Tenían que aguardarse que se acabara la calor y todo, porque planchaban en la noche o en la madrugada. Estaban planchando muy tarde en la noche, y loo es que le dijo mamá a mi hermana,

—¡Sabes qué? Que me da muncho miedo con tal y tal persona porque dicen que es bruja.

Y loo se quedaron un ratito asina y es que lloró un coyote en la canal, en frente de la puerta, y dijo mi mamá,

—¡Yo no supe ni de la plancha! Yo dejé la plancha conforme y nos acostamos muy calladitas, yo y Adelaida.

Toavía está mi hermana. Ella puede dijir lo mismo o puede dijir más mejor que yo, porque ellas, mis otras hermanas, eran las que estaban levantadas y vieron y escucharon lo que pasó. Pus yo era muy miedosa. Yo ya estaba acostada.

108

En otra vez estábanos aquí en esa casa ahi onde vive el Luis. Ahi vivía la dijunta Rebeca. Pus antes se pasiaban los vecinos unos con otros. En las tardes salían. Y loo nojotros medianos nos juntábanos a jugar. Me acuerdo que dicía mi mamá paá pa las laderas había visto tres brasas y que iban saltando. Yo no poo dijir muncho porque me dio tanto miedo que mejor ya no quise ni oír ni ver ni nada, pero ellas, las mujeres, estaban platicando ahí en el patio. Dijo mamá que habían visto tres brasas saltando ahi, que habían subido un cañoncito.

Emelinda Gonzales

A Coyote Howled

My mom used to talk about that sort of thing also, about a neighbor of theirs. She lived around here close by, here in Guache. She and my sister Adelaida one time were ironing at night, because a long time ago they used irons you heated on top of the stove. They ironed at night or in early morning when it was cool. Once they were ironing real late in the evening, and then my mom said to my sister:

"Do you know what? I'm very much afraid of so-and-so because they say she's a witch."

And then they remained quiet for a moment and about that time a coyote howled on top of the canal, right in front of the door, and my mom said:

"I forgot all about the iron! I left the iron just as it was, and we went to bed very quietly, Adelaida and I."

My sister's still alive. She can tell you the same thing, perhaps even better than I, because they're the ones, my other sisters, who were still up and they saw and heard what happened. I was very much of a chicken. I was already in bed.

On another occasion we were here in that house where Luis lives. That's where the late Rebeca lived. Well, a long time ago neighbors went out in the evening for a stroll. And then those of us who were small would get together to play. I remember that my mom would recall that on up the hills she had seen three balls of fire, and that they were jumping up and down. I can't say too much about it because I got so scared that I didn't even want to hear or see anything, but that's what the women were talking about there in the patio. My mom said that they had seen three balls of fire jumping about, and that they had gone up a small canyon.

Emelinda Gonzales

Se murió de mal ojo

Yo oía muncho del mal ojo. Y llegué a ver que dicían que sanaba una criatura cuando vinía la persona que le hizo ojo a darle agua. Si no, pus que no iba a sanar.

Creí en el mal ojo porque mi cuñada dice que la muchita que ella tuvo se murió de mal ojo. Ella tuvo una mujercita nomás y ella dice que de mal ojo se murió. La llevó a retratar y que allá en la retratería dice ella que esta persona la encantó. Muncho la vido y le gustó muncho y que cuando vinieron de allá de Las Vegas, que ya la muchita vino mala y ya no descansó y no descansó.

Y que estaba, como dicían, que con el mal ojo empezaban a voltiar el estógamo, los chiquitos. La mamá dice que empezó diuna vez a estar mala asina. No tenía nada cuando la llevó a la retratería. Y la tiene retratada.

La mamá dice que deso se murió esa muchita. Y la retrataron. Hasta se me hace que en un cojín de panea colorao. Se me hace que está atrás de ella, y loo muy bonita la muchita.

Sí llegué a ver cuando estaba más mediana que iban y traiban a tal y tal persona pa que viniera a curar al niño o niña porque estaban malos. Sería o no sería cierto pero nojotros oíanos eso.

Emelinda Gonzales

She Died from the Evil Eye

I used to hear a lot about the evil eye. And I heard that a child would get well when the person who had inflicted the evil eye came and gave it water. If the person didn't come to give it water, well, then it didn't get well.

I believed in the evil eye because my sister-in-law says that her child died from the evil eye. She had only this one, a little girl, and she claims that her daughter died from the evil eye. She took her to have her photographed, and at the photography shop this person enchanted her. She looked at her and admired her a lot, and when they returned from Las Vegas, the little girl was already ill. She simply didn't get well.

As they used to say, she was suffering from the evil eye because, like other children, she was beginning to vomit. Her mother says that the child started getting sick right away, but that there wasn't anything wrong with her when she took her to the photography shop. And she's got a picture of her.

Her mother says that that's what the little girl died from. And they photographed her. She was sitting on a red velvet cushion or I believe it's behind her; the little girl was very pretty.

While I was young I did get to see that people would go and get such-and-such a person so that she'd come and tend to the little boy or girl because they were ill with the evil eye. Whether it was true or not is another matter, but we used to hear about it.

Emelinda Gonzales

Filomena M. Gonzales

FILOMENA M. GONZALES

Nació: El 11 de agosto, 1910
Tecolote, NM
Entrevista: El 23 de junio, 1989
Sena, NM
Fallecida

Born: August 11, 1910
Tecolote, NM
Interview: June 23, 1989
Sena, NM
Deceased

Vamos a subirnos todos en el burro

Éste era el cuento de este viejito y vivía ahí en el Tecolote, en la placita de abajo onde vivíanos nojotros. Y todas las tardes se juntaba aá, dionde [había] más viejitos, onde vivían mis agüelitos, a contar cuentos. Dicía él,

—Cuando yo era niño éranos muy terribles. ¡Lo terrible que éranos!

Un día aquí en el Tecolote había munchos burros. Ahi se mantenían en los basuderos royendo ololotes y garras que tiraba la gente. Yo notaba que loo entre nojotros había una parranda de niños allá jugando y pus es que le habían dicho ellos [al viejito],

—Vamos a subirnos todos en el burro.

Es que empezaron a subirse, subirse, subirse, y eran munchos. Y es que entre más se subían, decía él [el viejito], más crecía el burro, más crecía el burro, hasta que se subieron casi todos. Y loo quedó el niño más chiquito y dijo,

—¿Y ónde me subo yo? Ya yo no quepo.

—Ahi quédate tú—le dijieron—. Después te subemos a ti solo.

—Güeno, pus que les vaya bien—es que les dijo el niño—.

—Píquenle la cruz pa que repare.

Y cuando les dijo "píquenle la cruz," es que *boom* hizo el burro y se desapareció. Se quedaron todos sentaos en el suelo.

114

Filomena M. Gonzales

Let's All Hop on the Donkey

This is the story about this little old man who lived in Tecolote, in the placita, down below where we lived. And every evening he went over where little old men mingled, where my grandparents lived, to tell stories. He used to say:

"When I was a little boy, we were real devilish. You should have seen how awful we were!"

One day there in Tecolote there was a whole lot of donkeys. They'd entertain themselves in the trash heaps chewing on corn cobs and rags that people would throw away. Then I noticed that among us children there was a bunch playing there who said to the little old man, "Let's all hop on the donkey."

They started climbing on one by one, and there were lots of them. The more that hopped on, according to the old man, the larger the donkey grew until almost all of them got on. Then the only one left was the smallest child and he said:

"And where do I get on? There's no room for me."

"Just stay put," they told him. "We'll put you on by yourself later on."

"Okay then, good luck to you." Then the child said to them:

"Prick him in the crotch so he'll buck."

And when he said "prick him in the crotch," the donkey went "boom" and he disappeared. And they were all left sitting on the ground.

Filomena M. Gonzales

Un agüelo

Aquí andaba gente también hablando de un agüelo, que es que les había salido a los hermanos de mi marido. Se habían ido su papá y su mamá a un viaje y lo habían dejao a él con sus hermanos, con sus hermanitas, en la noche. Es que tenían ellas tanto miedo que no solo, ¿ves? Muy temprano es que metieron leña y de todo y cerraron las puertas de su casa antes de que se hiciera oscuro porque ahí cerca vivía l'agüelo y luego él, mi marido, no tenía miedo. Él tenía muncho valor. Es que les dijo a sus hermanitos,

—Demen los asadores.

Prendían un horno, desos que iban en la pader. Pusieron los asadores los que usaban pa asar carne. Los pusieron como en las brasas, a calentarse, y ahi es que los calentaron hasta que estaban aquellos asadores bien calientitos. Cuando a güenas horas ahi viene aquel gallo, el agüelo, con munchos cortes que hasta colgaban las pajuelas y que les tocaba la puerta y ellos no querían abrir. Al fin abrieron. Ahi vinía con aquel pajo de lazos que le retumbaban las pajuelas. Isque dijía,

—¡Curucú! Baila la Paloma conmigo [a una de las hermanitas], y si no la bailas, báilala tú [a otra hermanita].

Quería que bailaran isque la Paloma con él. ¡Qué Paloma, ni Paloma! Ellos que estaban más fasinaos que otra cosa con su traje.

Y loo es que mi agüelo entró cuando le abrieron aquéllos la puerta al agüelo. Se metió tras de la puerta y lo dejó que entrara el agüelo pallá dentro. Traiba un cuero como de cíbolo y acá en la cabeza, con cascabeles. Es que le prendió mi agüelo los cascabeles asina. ¡Uh! Era una bola de juego. Y salió el agüelo volao pa juera. Aá juera tiró los cueros. Ni de los cueros se acordó. Se jue. No más golvió a mi casa.

—¿No estuve—dijo mi agüelo—más malo que el agüelo? (Risas).

Después de muncho tiempo es que le platicaron que el agüelo era un tío dél.

Filomena M. Gonzales

A Bogeyman

There was a story about a bogeyman who used to roam these parts and rumor has it that he sneaked up on my husband's brothers and sisters. Their mom and dad had gone on a trip and had left him one night with his brothers and sisters, who were quite young. I guess they were scared out of their wits. Very early in the evening they gathered firewood and everything, and they locked the doors before it got dark because the bogeyman lived nearby, but my husband wasn't afraid. He was very brave. He said to them:

"Give me the skewers."

They were accustomed to lighting up the *horno* [a beehive oven], those that you find in the wall, and they put the skewers, the kind you use to roast meat, on the coals so they would get nice and hot. All of a sudden, at just the right moment, there comes that devil, the bogeyman, with lots of shaggy rags and sulphur matches hanging down his sides. I understand that he was knocking on the door, but the children didn't want to answer. Finally they opened the door. There he was with straw-like tassels that caused the matches to make a rumbling noise. He would repeat:

"Coo! Coo! Come do the Pigeon Dance with me, my little one (talking to one of the sisters), and if she doesn't, you do it."

The bogeyman wanted them to do the Pigeon Dance. What Pigeon Dance! The children were more mesmerized by his appearance than anything else.

Then I understand grandpa entered when the others opened the door for the bogeyman. Grandpa got behind the door and he let the bogeyman way inside the house. The bogeyman was wearing like a bison's hide on his head, plus snake rattles. I understand that grandpa set fire to the snake rattles. Wow! It was a ball of fire. The bogeyman flew outside, where he shed his hides and forgot to take them with him. He just took off and never came back to my house.

"Wasn't I meaner than the bogeyman?" said grandpa. (Laughter).

A long time afterwards, according to people's gossip, they told him that the bogeyman was an uncle of his.

Filomena M. Gonzales

Rosendo Gonzales

ROSENDO GONZALES

Nació: el 3 de mayo, 1910
Sena, NM
Entrevista: El 23 de junio, 1989
Sena, NM

Born: May 3, 1910
Sena, NM
Interview: June 23, 1989
Sena, NM

No tenía cara

Pus a mí me pescó la Llorona. Me pescó y ya me iba a llevar. Era [tenía] como unos ocho años y andábanos jugando aá abajo. Yo vivía aá arriba juntra la iglesia, de la capilla, pero de aá me venía a jugar con los sobrinos aquí abajo, ahi donde vive mi primo. Ahi mero nos salió.

Pus andábanos aá en la cequia, ya descalzos, adentro de l'agua y todo eso, cuando menos pensamos salió de aá. De aá vinía con un chicote pero largo. Pus era una cosa muy feya, y nomás la vimos nosotros y arrancamos. A mí ya mero, ya mero me pescaba, y yo me vine descalzo, sin zapatos, sin todo eso, porque si me volvía patrás me pescaba, ¿ves?

Pues así le hicimos y salimos ajuir todos. Éranos como cuatro o cinco que andábanos ahi. Y nos vinimos, nomás que pus mi hermana vivía ahí cerquita, en esa casa ahi onde ellos florean, y pescamos pa dentro de la casa.

Pus de aquí me tuve que ir yo paá par onde vivía yo paá arriba, y loo me dicen en papá y mamá,

—¿Pus qué pasó con los zapatos? No traes zapatos.

—Pus aá los dejé porque ya me agarraba la Llorona.

Tuve que salir a juir. Me acuerdo. Se vía una cosa muy, muy horrible. No tenía cara. Pus sí tenía, ves, pero quizás traiba alguna cosa puesta, sabes cómo. Tapaba la cara y eso, pero se vía una cosa muy horrible, y nojotros nomás la vimos, se nos hizo largo el camino de ahí. ¡Nomás a la casa! Y no pueden ser más de como unos cien, doscientos pies cuando más.

120

Rosendo Gonzales

It Didn't Have a Face

Well, the Wailing Woman got a hold of me. She caught me and she was about to take me with her. I was about eight years old. We were playing down below my house. I lived up above close to the church, by the chapel, but I'd come from up there to play with my nephews down here, there where my cousin lives. Right there is where the Wailing Woman popped out at me.

Well, we were over by the ditch, barefoot, in the water and all, when all of a sudden she came out. There she was, headed our way carrying a whip, but long. She was a very ugly thing, and all we did was look at her and we took off. And she was about to catch me, and I headed home barefoot, without shoes, without anything, because if I turned back she would catch me, right?

That's what we did; we all took off. There were about four or five of us who were together. And we headed home. The only thing is that my sister lived right there close by, in that home where they sift flour, and we headed inside the house.

From here I had to take off to where I lived up the hill, and then my mom and dad said to me:

"Well what happened to your shoes? You're not wearing any shoes."

"Well I left them down there because the Wailing Woman was about to catch me."

I had to take off running. I remember. You could see a very, very horrible (ugly) thing. It didn't have a face. Well, it did have one, you see, but perhaps it was wearing something to cover her face. You know what I mean. It covered her face and more, but you could see a very ugly thing, and no sooner did we see it than we headed for home! The road home seemed quite long, but I'm sure it's no more than a 100, 200 feet at the very most.

Rosendo Gonzales

Salía el agüelo todas las noches

¡Uh! Si yo me acuerdo que a mí, aá onde vivíanos nojotros—como unas tres casas pallá—ahi salía el agüelo todas las noches. No podías salir tú la puerta porque diuna vez ahi está ya.

Y luego íbanos nojotros pa case mi agüelo y, ¡pus qué podías ir! No podías ir porque aquel gallo ondequiera salía, y loo traiba un chicotote desos largos, y nomás le traquiaba a uno asina y tenías que salir ajuir.

Había veces que cuasi nomás en cuanto no lo agarraba a uno antes de entrar a la casa. Y ése era todas las noches; si no era nomás una vez. De noche no podías tú salir. No. El agüelo siempre estaba ahí en un ladito.

Y jugábanos tamién a las carreras aá, de aquel lao del camposanto ese que tenemos ahi. Ahi nos salió el agüelo tamién. Éranos un bonche que estáanos paquel lao del camposanto. Toavía está un cerco asina de ésos de pulla. Güeno, pus, cuando andábanos allá, era en la noche. Nomás en la noche íbanos pallá y nos quitábanos los zapatos y loo corríanos descalzos. Teníanos las veredas hechas muy limpiecitas y todo. No estaban en el zacate. Las hacíanos del propio y ahi estáanos jugando una noche, corriendo, y nos quitábanos los pantalones y nos quedábanos en *shorts*. (Risas). Pus ahi tienes tú que esa noche éranos como veinte los que habíanos de plebe y subieron dos agüelos de aquí de Sena. De aquí subieron el Portecito y empezaron hacernos,

—¡Rucucú! ¡Rucucú!

Y no los habíanos visto hasta que no entraron la puerta del camposanto pallá, y nojotros estábanos paquel lao. Y ahi estaba el cerco del camposanto y logo estaba el cerco este otro que les digo aá atrás. Pus qué, nomás entraron pallá y pensamos que no iban ir pallá, pero sí jueron. Como vían que no nos movíanos, pues ahi tienes tú que nomás pasaron la mitá del camposanto pallá y, ¡híjole la patada! ¡Salimos a juir todos! Y del puro miedo que tráibanos, tiramos hasta el cerco ese otro que estaba acá. Le pegamos todos juntos. Los rasguños por aquí, por ondequiera. ¡Todos rasguñaos!

Rosendo Gonzales

The Bogeyman Would Come Out Every Night

Wow! I remember that, over where we lived about three houses on up like that—that's where the bogeyman would come out every night. You couldn't even step outside the door because all of a sudden, there he was.

And whenever we wanted to go to my grandpa's house, don't you know, we couldn't because that devil would pop out just about everywhere, and then, to top it all off, he was carrying one of those long, thick whips, and all he had to do was crack it like so in front of you and you'd take off running.

There were times when he barely missed you as you were about to get inside the house. And that was every night; it wasn't just one night. At night you just couldn't go out. You couldn't. The bogeyman was always right there, waiting for you.

We also had foot races there, on the other side of that cemetery. The bogeyman also sneaked up on us right there. There was a bunch of us who were there on the other side of the cemetery. It was fenced in with one of those barbed-wire fences. It was night when we were hanging around up there. We only went there at night and we'd take off our shoes and then we'd race barefoot. We had the trails cut out, very neat and all. They weren't on the grass. We'd cut them out where we wanted them and that's where we were playing one night, running actually. We'd taken off our pants and there we were in shorts. (Laughter). As luck would have it, that night there were about 20 of us kids, and two bogeymen came up from Sena. From there they climbed el Portecito and they started making noises:

"Rucucú! Rucucú!"

And we hadn't seen them until they went in the gate to the cemetery up that way, and we were on the other side. That's where the cemetery fence was, and then there was this other fence on the other side. No sooner had they (the bogeymen) gone in that way, and we thought that they weren't going to head our way, but they did. Being that they didn't see us move, well, wouldn't you know it, they go halfway past the cemetery, and damn! We all took off running! And just from being afraid, we knocked down that other fence that was over this way. We all ran into it at the same time. Scratches here and there and everywhere. We were nothing but scratches!

Rosendo Gonzales

Isidoro V. Lucero, Jr.

Isidoro V. Lucero, Jr.

Nació: El 22 de agosto, 1915
Villanueva, NM
Entrevista: El 11 de julio, 1993
Villanueva, NM
Fallecido

Born: August 22, 1915
Villanueva, NM
Interview: July 11, 1993
Villanueva, NM
Deceased

Les habían hecho mal

Mi tío Vicente de Villanueva era un contador. Y lego, Mamelita también contaba, pero no era muy graciosa como mi tío Vicente. Pero el que contaba mejor era ese hombre Severo, pienso, o mi tío Vicente, uno de los dos.

Pos aquí también platicaban muncho de un hermano de Rafel Salinas. Déjame ver si me acuerdo cómo se llamaba. No lo conocí yo. No sé cómo se llamaba, pero era Salinas. Él se metía abajo el arroyo y salía metiéndole miedo a la gente que era ladrona, hasta que la plebe le perdió el miedo.

Mamelita platicaba que—yo creo que ahi onde le dicen el Torreón—ahi atrás había algunas casitas. Ahi vivía un hombre de Villanueva. Déjame ver. Se me hace que se llamaba Vicente también, pero no era mi tío Vicente de los cuentos, pero el papá de él. Ése reclamaban que le habían hecho mal en la brujería.

Y loo es que jue y se le puso muy nojón él a la mujer, su esposa, y le dijo que la iba matar si no lo curaba de las narices asina grandotas.

—¡Y no tienes nada!—es que le dijía.

—Pues mira, si no me sanas ...

Y es que le echaba reniegos él. Loo vino ella y nomás agarró ceniza del fogón y le untó y descansó él.

Que será verdá, no sé, pero asina platicaban.

Otra vez me acuerdo que me platicaba mi papá de un hombre, de un señor que le hicieron mal las brujas. Luego cuando iba en el camino se le hincharon muncho las narices y agarró un palo él, un garrote. Se jue pa la mujer que le había hecho el mal y llegó a la casa y loo le dijo que le abriera, y no quería abrile y al fin le abrió. Pero cuando iba en el camino isque se le atravesaban tecolotes y quién sabe qué tanto. Loo isque le dijo,

—¡Me abres!—y le echó una palabra mala y le abrió y luego quería que lo curara, que sanara.

—Pus si no tienes nada—isque le dicía.

Y loo vino, y tenía un fogón de tierra, y agarró ceniza y la mojó y la untó en las narices y sanó. Eso me platicaba en papá. A él le platicaron. Él mesmo no lo vido.

Isidoro V. Lucero, Jr.

Someone Bewitched Them

My uncle Vicente from Villanueva was a storyteller. And then, Mamelita also told stories, but she was not as funny as my uncle Vicente. But the one who really narrated stories was a man named Severo, I believe, or my own uncle Vicente, one of the two.

Around these parts people also used to talk a lot about a brother of Rafael Salinas. Let me see if I can remember what his name was. I never knew him. No, I don't know what his name was, but he was a Salinas. He used to hide down in the arroyo and he'd come out to scare away thieves, until sooner or later the kids were no longer afraid of him.

Mamelita used to say that—I believe that it was that place people called el Torreón—right behind it there were some small houses. That's where this man from Villanueva lived. Let me see. I believe his name was also Vicente, but it wasn't my uncle Vicente, the one who told stories, but his father instead or something like that. Rumor has it that someone had put a curse on him.

Then I understand he went home and got very mean with his wife and he told her that he was going to kill her if she didn't cure him of the oversized nose he had developed.

"Why there's nothing wrong with you!" she'd say to him.

"Well listen, if you don't get me well . . ."

He'd curse her no end, so she went and all she did was to fetch some ashes from the potbellied stove and applied them to his nose and he got well.

Whether it's true or not, I don't know, but that's what people used to say.

Another time I remember my father telling me about a man, a gentleman who had been bewitched. When this man was on the road his nose swelled up a lot and he grabbed a stick, a cudgel. He headed for the home of the woman who had bewitched him. He arrived at her house and implored her to open the door and she didn't want to, but finally she did. But whenever he traveled on the road, so goes the story, owls and who knows what else would get in front of him. Then he supposedly said to her, "Open up!" and he swore at her. She opened the door for him and he wanted her to

Isidoro V. Lucero, Jr.

Y una otra vez que jui a un *play* a Pecos y luego cuando allá me empezaron a salir como munchas ronchas. Ya se me hinchó muncho la boca. Me amarró un trapo ahi, y loo me llevó a un arbolario, mi madrastra, y jue y se me quitó. Todo lo que le dijo nomás, que me pusiera agua serrenal en las ventanas y luego que viniera un muchito chiquito que me pusiera la cruz. Y ahi estoy. Se me quitó. No más me volvió.

Y la razón por qué me dijo el niño es que yo le había prometido algunas dos mujeres más casarme con ellas y loo me escapé. Creía que ésas me habían hecho mal.

Isidoro V. Lucero, Jr.

cure him, to get him well.

"Why there's nothing wrong with you," she kept saying to him.

But she went—she had an adobe fireplace—and grabbed some ashes, wet them and rubbed them on his nose and he got well. That's what my dad used to tell me. That's what they told him. He himself did not see it.

On another occasion I went to a play in Pecos and then while there I started getting lots of welts. My mouth really swelled up. My stepmother applied a cloth to the welts and then took me to an herbalist and the swelling went away. All the herbalist did was to tell her to put mountain water on the windowsills and then for a little boy to come and make the sign of the cross, for him to bless me. And there you are. It went away. The spell never came back.

And the reason for my trouble, the little boy told me, is that I supposedly promised a couple of women that I would marry them and then I copped out. He thought that they were the ones who had bewitched me.

129

Isidoro V. Lucero, Jr.

Rosavé M. Lucero

ROSAVÉ M. LUCERO

Nació: El 3 de noviembre, 1914
Villanueva, NM
Entrevista: El 29 de junio, 1989
Villanueva, NM

Born: November 3, 1914
Villanueva, NM
Interview: June 29, 1989
Villanueva, NM

Era de estos mujereros

Me acuerdo que nos contaban los viejitos de antes munchos [cuentos], pero no me acuerdo bien ni los nombres ni todo. Pero me acuerdo deste que nos contaban.

Cuando me casé yo me platicaba la agüelita de mi esposo, deste hombre acabao de casarse que salía muncho de noche. No era muy güeno salirse de noche cuando ya se casaba uno, pero tenía esa moda. A la mujer no le contaba él par onde iba ni nada y salía a caballo él muy *nice*. Y ella no se quejaba, por sus suegros.

Este hombre salía tanto que, asegún mi agüelita, que ahi en Sena—antes le dicían el Puertecito—en frente de los álamos, iba él en el caballo cuando se detuvo poco el caballo. Isque oyó él como el llanto de un bebito y voltió par dionde venía el ruido onde estaba llorando. Isque vido un bebito él en el suelo, tirao. Le dio como muncho temor, pero siempre isque dijo,

—¡Cómo lo voy a dejar tirao!

Paró el caballo pa apiarse pa ver si era lo que estaba viendo y cuando voltió que iba apiarse estaba el muchito, el bebito, atrás dél en las anancas. Voltió el hombre y se quedó otra vez viéndole y isque le dijo el bebito,

—Tengo dientes. Tengo dientes.

Le dio tanto temor al hombre, que el bebé se espantó y despareció. Y la agüelita dicía [que] no era otro más del diablo porque no estaba haciendo cosas, *an honest living* [el esposo] con su mujer.

De todos modos, se mendó tanto el hombre que no más volvió porque era destos mujereros que iba a ver mujeres, seguro, y lego ya no volvió más hacer esto.

Rosavé M. Lucero

He Was One of These Womanizers

Well, I remember that the old folks used to tell us a lot of stories, but I don't recall very well the names or anything. But I remember this one that they used to tell us.

When I got married my husband's grandma would tell me about this recently married man who used to go out a lot at night. You see, it wasn't a good idea to go catting around at night after you got married, but this man had that habit. He would never tell his wife where he was going or anything, and he'd take off on horseback looking very nice. And of course she didn't complain, because of her in-laws.

One time when he went out, according to my grandma, there in front of some trees in Sena—Sena used to be called El Puertecito—the horse slowed down and he heard the crying of a baby. He turned around in the direction where the crying noise was coming from. People say that he saw a baby on the ground, abandoned. He got very scared, but I guess he said to himself: "How can I leave it there?"

He stopped his horse to see if it's what he thought it was, and when he turned around to get down, there was the little boy, the baby, already behind him on the horse's rump. The man turned around and the baby, staring at him, said to him:

"I have teeth. I have teeth."

The man got so scared that he startled the baby and it disappeared. And the grandma claimed that it had to be the devil, because the husband wasn't involved in anything good, like earning an honest living to support his wife.

Anyway, I guess the husband mended his ways, so that he never went out again carrying on as a womanizer. For sure from that time on he never did that, ever again.

133

Rosavé M. Lucero

Antonia A. Ortiz

ANTONIA A. ORTIZ

Nació: El 31 de julio, 1912
La Lagunita, NM
Entrevista: El 4 de marzo, 1993
El Pueblo, NM

Born: July 31, 1912
La Lagunita, NM
Interview: March 4, 1993
El Pueblo, NM

Vide yo la lucecita

Yo no me acuerdo más de que una luz aparecía aquí en esta lomita. Bajaba redonda, y una noche que estaba yo esperando a mi hijo, que venía de allá de Téxaco, me asusté. Y vide yo la lucecita que venía. Venía rodando asina como una tapaderita. Se vían bien, bien las piedritas. Y ahi se paró. Yo no sé qué pasaría con ella.

Pero una viejita que vivía ahi, que taa están las ruinas de la casa de ella, me platicaba a mí que es que planchaba ropa y tenía la idea de ila poniendo arriba la cama—la ropa que planchaba. Y en la noche que iba ella a recoger la ropa, la luz es que andaba arriba de la cama. Y platicaba esa mujer, es que llegaron a ver en el soterrano esa luz.

Es que una vez vinieron dos hombres ahi. Porque ella dicía que es que tenía oro; había oro molido entre la piedra ahi, en el soterrano. Es que llevaron dos cajoncitos asina de tierra. Y le prometieron a ella volver y dicile qué habían sacao, pero no volvieron. Es que oro molido, dicían.

Yo no sé. Yo nomás eso vide. ¡Oh! Su papá de esta muchacha, es que vido una luz. Una raya asina, que vinía del camino, pacá abajo estendido, que se atravezó, como una raya asina adelante de él. No jallaba cómo pasar. Tenía miedo. Que cuando llegó a la casa pus es que se desmayó. Le dio muncho miedo. Pus nunca supieron qué eran esas luces ni nada.

Y esa viejita que te digo yo que dicía que había oro molido ahi, me dicía a mí que entre medio de esa casa, esa *pink* que está ahi, es que había una tapia. Y dice ella que es que hay un tesoro enterrao. ¡Sabrá Dios!

¡Ooohh! Otra cosa que te iba dicir yo. Mi tío Miguel es que enterró dinero por aquí, porque dicían que era en los Cañoncitos de los Riberas. Yo creo que es ese arroyo que viene ahi, porque aquí eran puros Riberas, porque su mamá de José [su esposo] era Ribera, y subía muncha gente, oye, a escarbar ahi. Nojotros llegamos ir paá y sí tenían pozos. Yo llegué a ir hasta con José pallá. Me dicía José:

Antonia A. Ortiz

I Saw the Shiny Little Light

I only remember that a light used to appear here at this little hill. It'd come rolling, and one night while I was waiting for my son, who was on his way back from Texaco, I got scared. I saw the shiny little light headed this way. It was rolling like this, like a small lid. You could see the pebbles really well. And it stopped right there. I don't know what happened to it.

But a little old lady who used to live there, whose house ruins are still there, she used to tell me herself that as she ironed clothes she'd put them on top of the bed. And at night when she was going to gather the clothes, the light would bounce around on top of the bed. That woman used to say that people would also see the light in the basement.

It is said that once two men went there. It so happens that gold could be found there, according to her; gold powder supposedly was mixed in with the rocks there in the basement. Apparently two small boxes full of dirt were taken from the basement and those involved promised to return to tell her what they had found, but they never came back. The gold was ground up, so said the people.

I don't know. I only saw the light. Oh, by the way. This girl's father also is said to have seen the light. A streak of light that was headed straight down part of the road, and it crossed like a ray of light right in front of him. He couldn't figure out a way to cross. He was scared. It seems he fainted when he got home. He was scared to death. Well, nobody ever found out what those lights were or anything.

And that little old lady I'm talking about, who said there was gold powder there, she used to tell me that there in between that house, the pink house that's there, that's where a wall once was. She used to say that there was a buried treasure there. God only knows!

Oooohh! Another thing I was going to tell you. My uncle Miguel, rumor has it, buried money around here, at a place called los Cañoncitos, that belongs to the Riberas. I believe it's that arroyo that runs through there, because only Riberas lived here, and José's mom [her husband's mother] was a Ribera, and listen, a lot of people would go up there to dig. We ourselves went and, sure enough,

137

Antonia A. Ortiz

—Pus vamos a ver si jallas tú el tesoro o lo jallo yo.

Nunca jallamos nada. Nomás que escarbaban muncho. Pero no, nunca jallamos nada. ¿Quién sabe? Pus quién sabe si ellos mesmos [los Ribera] vendrían a ver si se lo llevarían. ¿Qué crees tú que no? Porque mi tío Miguel se jue de aquí. Puede que él se lo llevaría.

Antonia A. Ortiz

there were holes that had been dug. I even got to go there with José. José used to say to me, "Well, let's see if you can find the treasure, or if I can find it."

We never found anything. The only thing we ever did was to dig a lot, but we never found a thing. Who knows? Who knows but what the Riberas themselves came and took it away. Don't you think so? Because Uncle Miguel left these parts. Perhaps he took it with him.

Antonia A. Ortiz

Clara S. Ortiz

CLARA S. ORTIZ

Nació: El 29 de marzo, 1912
San José, NM
Entrevista: El 29 de mayo, 1990
San José, NM

Born: March 29, 1912
San José, NM
Interview: May 29, 1990
San José, NM

Una manzana atrás dél

Pues yo oí una vez que este hombre estaba embrujado, y un arbolario lo curó. Porque es que una manazana andaba todo el tiempo atrás dél. Isque el embrujado se hacía bola y se metía abajo de las silletas. Era la brujería. Y este arbolario, ya hasta está muerto el hombre, pero lo curó y le dijo,

—Si tú haces lo que yo te mando, te curo. La mujer que te hizo mal era de San Juan, de por ahi de San Juan. La que te hizo mal está como dos millas y media de aquí.

Era en el Ancón, la mujer que le había hecho mal. Y lo curó, con remedios, con hierbas dél.

Esta cosa lo siguía, y era como en forma de manzana, quizás, porque le hacía muy mal. Lo hacía meterse es que abajo de una silleta; hecho bolita lo hacía caber ahi. Es que muy atroz, se platicaba. Eso sí lo oía decir yo de brujerías.

A mí me hicieron ojo en el cabello

Y de ojo, a mí me hicieron ojo en el cabello. Una vez, cuando comenzaba el *perm*, jui a Pecos. Vivía una gente de aquí en San José, aá, familias ahi de nosotros. Y les dije aquí,

—Yo me voy ir pa Pecos hacerme un *perm*. Al cabo aá tengo onde llegar y no vengo hasta mañana.

Pus sí, me jui. Román, mi esposo, no estaba aquí; estaba trabajando lejos. *Anyway* que me jui y me hice un *perm*. Y luego me jue creciendo el cabello, que jue cuando iba nacer Roberto, m'hijo. Él nació ora en setiembre, el día ocho. Ya tenía tan largo el cabello. Se me iba saliendo, pero yo siempre he tenido un *natural curler*. No me gusta. Y me hago *perm*. El cuento es que ya lo tenía tan largo, y lo tenía *brownish*, muy bonito cabello tenía. Ya me daba aquí a la cintura, pero todavía poquito *perm* en l'orilla, y no me lo cortó la mujer.

Me hicieron ojo y se me cayó el cabello aquí mero en la frente.

Clara S. Ortiz

An Apple Was Chasing Him

Well, I heard it said once that this man was bewitched, and an herbalist got him well. I understand that an apple was constantly chasing him. I'm told the bewitched man would turn into a ball, and he'd get underneath the chairs. It was witchcraft. And this herbalist, he's already dead, he cured him, but he told him:

"If you do as I tell you, I'll get you well. The woman who put a spell on you is from San Juan, somewhere around San Juan. The woman who bewitched you is about two and a half miles from here."

She was from Ancón, the lady who had bewitched him. But he got him well with herbal remedies.

This thing would follow him, and it was in the shape of an apple, and it would really get him sick. The apple would force the man under a chair and, by turning him into a tiny ball, he'd fit under there. It was awful, according to people who talked about it. That's one thing I used to hear said about witches.

Someone Cast a Spell on My Hair

And speaking of the evil eye, someone cast a spell on my hair. Once, when perms were becoming fashionable, I went to Pecos. Some people from here in San José lived over there, relatives of ours. And I told them here:

"I'm going to Pecos to get a perm. Anyway, I have a place to stay there, so I won't be back until tomorrow."

So I took off. My husband Román wasn't here; he was working far away. Anyway, I went and I got a perm. Then my hair started growing. This was when my son Roberto was about to be born. He was born on September the eighth. My hair was really getting long. It kept growing, but I have always had a natural curl. I don't like it. So I get a perm. In any case, my hair was really long, and it was brownish, very beautiful hair. It came down to my waist, but it still had a little curl at the end, so the lady didn't cut it.

Then someone cast an evil-eye spell on my hair and it fell out

Clara S. Ortiz

Bien parecía que con la navaja de barba se me había cortado bien lisito. Me dieron el remedio de que juera con un Juan o una Juanita, que me escupiera tres viernes a la misma hora, con la cachana. Es una raiz, y ésa la quemaba, la que iba curar a uno, y l'agarraba en la boca y la molía cuando ya la quemaba. Y luego le escupía a uno a la misma hora tres viernes. Me salió cabello.

Por pura envidia de mi cabello alguien me hizo ojo y no sabiendo quién lo va curar uno, pero me dijieron que un Juan o una Juanita. Mujer o hombre, lo que tuviera más confianza. Mi tía Juanita Tafoya vivía aquí en San José, por ahi onde vivía mi comadre Manuelita. Jui y le hablé.

—¡Seguro que sí! Trae cachana, y yo te curo, pero tres viernes a la misma hora tienes que venir pa escupirte con la cachana.

Pus sí, hice como me mandó, ¿y sabes tú que me curó mi tía Juanita?

El empacho

Una vez se me empachó m'hija, la que vive hora en Alburquerque. Estaba [tenía] quizás como cuatro años. ¡Oh! No nos dejaba dormir en la noche. Llora y llora y que no quería comer, y la llevábanos al dotor. Nomás que le dolía la panza.

Y la llevamos a un doctor que en ese tiempo estaba muy joven. Estaba trabajando mi esposo, Román, ahi en el Dead Horse Ranch de por ahi. El cuento es que la llevamos y dijo el dotor,

—Pus en el estógamo tiene algo, pero yo no sé qué será—pero le dio una medecina.

L'empacho se cría en una tripa; ahi es onde se cría. L'agua, los dulces, y munchas comidas tamién son malas, pero los dulces y l'agua son los más malos pal empacho. Eso sí tengo yo por esperencia.

Vino Román y dijo,

—Yo voy a llamar a mi tío Manuel Sánchez.

Y como uno es media corta cuando está joven dije,

Clara S. Ortiz

right here above my forehead. It looked like they had cut it very smooth with a straight razor. I was advised to seek treatment from a Juan or a Juanita, for him or her to spit on me three successive Fridays at the same time, but using *cachana*. It's a root, and the person who's supposed to cure you would toast it, put it in her mouth and chew it. Then she would spit on your hair at the same time for three Fridays in a row. My hair grew back out.

Just because of pure jealousy for my hair, someone had cast the evil-eye spell on it, and then there's the question of who's going to get you well, but I was told that a Juan or a Juanita could do it. A woman or a man, whomever I had most confidence in. My aunt Juanita Tafoya lived around here in San José, right close to where my *comadre* Manuelita lived. I went and spoke to her.

"Why of course! Bring me some *cachana*, and I'll get you well, but for three Fridays in a row you have to come so I can spit *cachana* on you."

Well, I did as she said, and do you know that my aunt Juanita cured me?

Indigestion

One time my daughter, the one who lives in Albuquerque, got indigestion. She was about four years old. Oh! She wouldn't let us sleep at night. She cried and cried and she didn't want to eat, so we took her to the doctor. Her stomach just kept hurting.

We took her to a doctor who was quite young at the time. My husband Román was working there at the Dead Horse Ranch, or someplace close by. The doctor said:

"She has something stuck in her stomach, but I don't know what it is." But he gave her some medicine.

The indigestion is born in the intestine and that's where it grows. Water, candy, and many other foods also are the cause, but candies and water are the worst ones for indigestion. That I know because of experience.

Román came home and he said, "I'm going to call my Uncle Manuel Sánchez."

And since you have a short fuse and can't hold back your

Clara S. Ortiz

—Eh, ¿qué sabe ese viejo?

Pero jue y lo llamó. No me hizo caso Román, y lo trujo.

—Oh hijita—y hacía las manos asina [se las frotaba] y que—mira nomás que eletrecidá tienen estas manos, pero orora sobo a tu hijita.

Yo nomás escuchaba. Güeno, la sobó en l'espinazo, y ella muy calladita se quedó. La sobó y le traquió l'espinazo, porque les traquea l'espinazo atrás. Munchas soban con un huevo. Yo nunca. Yo sobo con la mano nomás y lego les jalo el cuero. Y le jaló el cuero mi tío Manuel y le traquió. Bien empachaba estaba la niña.

Güeno, no acababa de salir mi tío Manuel sin que no pidió que comer Román porque no había comido desde que llegó del Dead Horse Ranch. A m'hijita le di atole porque es güeno pal estómago.

—¿Qué te dije Clara? ¿Está bien el viejo o no?—me la cantó Román.

Pero muy bien que puse atención. Y luego mi mamá tamién sobaba pal empacho. Pus de ahi aprendí y me enseñé y yo sobaba. A mí me traiban de ahi de San Juan, me traiban unas muchitas seguido con todo tipo de empachada. Y las sobaba.

146

—¿Y cuánto me va cobrar?—cuando ya acababa.

—No, el remedio no se vende—les dicía yo. —Nomás que sanen y ahi estuvo.

Les sobaba primero, ¿vez? Ahi les sobaba hasta que se les aflojaba quizás l'empacho y loo le jalaba el cuero y si no traquea, no están empachaos. Tiene que traquiar, cuando jale uno el cuero. Se quejan los pobres niños, pus duele, porque cuando traquea, es que se desprendió l'empacho. Y les daba una cuchadarita de añil con sal, pero muncha sal, y pronto un vaso de agua. Y esa les hace purga pa desechar l'empacho. Más tarde usaba l'azogue.

Clara S. Ortiz

tongue when you're young, I said to him:

"Humbug! What does that old man know?"

But he went and called on him. Román didn't pay any attention to me. He brought him to the house. "Oh my little one," and he would rub his hands this way and that way. "Why, look at the electricity in my hands. I'll massage your precious daughter in just a little bit."

All I could do was listen. Well, he massaged her back, and she remained very silent. He massaged her and her back cracked, because that's what happens to your back. Many times they'll rub you with an egg. I never did that. I only rub with my hands and then I pull the skin. I pull the skin and I snap it. The child had quite a case of indigestion.

Well, no sooner had Uncle Manuel come and gone when Román asked for something to eat because he hadn't eaten since he had arrived from the Dead Horse Ranch. For my daughter I made her some *atole*, blue-corn gruel, which is good for your stomach.

"What did I tell you, Clara? The old man's okay, isn't he?" So said Román, rubbing it in.

And it's a good thing I paid close attention. My mother also gave massages for indigestion. That's how I learned and so I taught myself. That's why I used to give massages. They would bring me these little girls, quite often in fact, from there in San Juan, with all types of indigestion. And I used to massage them.

"And how much are you going to charge me?" they'd say to me after I finished.

"No. One doesn't sell the remedy," I used to tell them. "All that's important is for the little girls to get well, and that's it."

I would massage them first, you see? I'd rub them until the indigestion would loosen up and then I'd snap the skin and if it didn't crack they weren't suffering from indigestion. The skin has to crack when you snap it. The poor children complained, because it hurt. When it cracks, it's because the indigestion (the ball) has cut loose from the intestine. After the massage I would give them a teaspoon full of bluing with salt, but a lot of salt, followed immediately with a glass of water. That serves as a good laxative so as to get rid of the indigestion. Later on I used to use quicksilver.

Clara S. Ortiz

Petrita Ortiz

PETRITA ORTIZ

Nació: El 27 de abril, 1903
Cebadilla, NM
Entrevista: El 13 de febrero, 1993
San Miguel, NM
Fallecida

Born: April 27, 1903
Cebadilla, NM
Interview: February 13, 1993
San Miguel, NM
Deceased

Se llenaba de greñas el plato

Pus, había un hombre ahi en San José que se llamaba Ambrosio. Y es que le hicieron mal en el chile. ¡Una mujer! Cada vez que le llevaba su mujer el chile, es que se llenaba de greñas el plato. Eso dicía él. Él se nojaba muncho con su mujer. Y ella se lo llevaba limpio de la estufa.

Al fin lo curó un alborlario y sanó, porque tamién había un hombre que curaba esas enfermedades. Lo curó con hierbas que usaban más antes.

Y otro que enbrujaron ahi en el Alcón, a ése le hicieron mal en los orines. Le hicieron mal; le hicieron mal. Isque hicieron un mono de los orines. Y loo cada vez de que querían [que] estuviera malo le ponían una alfiler al mono. Le clavaban una alfiler al mono y ahi estaba él muriéndose. ¡Muriéndose estaba!

Pus al fin lo curaron tamién y descansó. ¡Y supo quién le hizo el mal! Supo hasta quién le había hecho el mal porque creo que el alborlario tenía idea.

150 Pus había algunos alborlarios ahi que curaban asina a ésos que se les hacían mal, que los enbrujaban. Dicían. Eso dicían.

Petrita Ortiz

The Plate Would Fill Up with Hair

Well, there was a man over in San José whose name was Ambrosio. And I understand that someone cast a spell on his chile. A woman! Every time his wife took him chile, the rumor has it that his plate would get full of hair. That's what he used to say. He would get real angry with his wife. And his wife used to take the plate to him clean from the stove.

Finally an herbalist cured him, and he got well, because there was this man who also treated those kinds of illnesses. He cured him with herbs that they used a long time ago.

And then there's another man there in Alcón whose urine was bewitched. They bewitched him, they bewitched him. Rumor has it that they made a rag doll from the urine. And every time that they wanted him to be ill they'd stick a pin in the doll. They'd stick a pin in the rag doll and there he was, suffering. He'd be dying!

Well, they finally cured him; he got well. And he found out who had bewitched him! He found out because I guess the herbalist somehow knew.

You see, there were some herbalists around who treated the victims of spells, who were bewitched. That's what people said anyway.

Petrita Ortiz

Se le caiban los dedos de los pies

Á en casa onde vivía yo, todo el tiempo dicían que es que andaba redondo de la iglesia una luz. Una chispa, una brasa, brasas, dicían ellas [las gentes]. La gente de allí creiba que eran las brujas. No, yo nunca las llegué a ver. Pero muncha gente sí dicía eso.

Un hombre vivía ahi junta de nosotros. Tamién ese hombre lo tenían quizás enbrujao porque había tiempos que estaba tan malo que no sólo. Y su mujer dicía que iba salir y las iba a pescar a las brujas y dales una güena zota. Tenía que ponerse el túnico al revés pa pescalas, pero nunca jue quizás porque al fin se murió él. Eso platicaban los vecinos que teníanos nojotros ahi onde vivíanos.

Tamién dicían igual unas vecinas que vivían ahi en junto de nosotros.

—Anoche andaba un cute largo ahi en la calle.

Nojotros nunca las llegamos a ver las brujas. Nunca, nunca. Pero las vecinas platicaban eso.

Y una mujer, se llamaba Petrita. Esa mujer padeció muncho tiempo, porque tenía llagas. Que se le caiban los dedos de los pies. Yo no sé qué tanto sería verdá o no sería, oiga, pero dicían que es que las brujas. Hasta que al fin se murió la pobre asina. Quizás no le hicieron naa pa curala.

A mí se me hace que no era brujería. Yo creo que era cáncer de ése que da ora. Se me hace a mí. Pero ellas dicían que las brujas, que las brujas la tenían asina, a muncha gente.

152

Petrita Ortiz

Her Toes Would Fall Off

Over where I lived, the word was going around all the time that a light could be seen circling the church. A spark, a red-hot coal, red-hot ashes, according to people. The people from around there thought those red-hot ashes were witches. No, I never saw them. But a lot of people swore they did.

There was a man who lived close to us. The witches also had him crazy, I guess, because there were times when he was so ill that he was beside himself. And his wife used to say that she was going to go out and catch the witches and give them a good whipping. She had to turn her dress inside out in order to catch them, but I guess she never did because he finally died. That's what the neighbors talked about there where we lived.

Some neighbors who used to live close to us also talked about it.

"Last night there was something in a long coat walking down the street."

We never got to see the witches. Never, never. But the neighbors used to talk about that.

And there was a woman named Petrita. That woman suffered a long time because she had sores. I understand that her toes would fall off. I don't know how much of it was true or not but, according to people, it was due to the witches. Finally the poor woman died after suffering from that illness. I guess they could never do anything for her.

I don't believe that it was witchcraft. I believe it was that cancer that's going around now. That's what I think. But the women would say that it was witches, that the witches had her in that state, as they did a lot of people.

Petrita Ortiz

José B. Quintana

JOSÉ B. QUINTANA

Nació: El 28 de julio, 1906
Las Vegas, NM
Entrevista: El 7 de enero, 1993
El Ranchito, NM

Born: July 28, 1906
Las Vegas, NM
Interview: January 7, 1993
El Ranchito, NM

San Antonio es muy milagroso

Hubo una historia ahi que me platicaba en papá, que San Antonio es muy milagroso. Le levantaron un crimen a su papá de San Antonio. Enterraron al difunto, que lo había matao otro hombre, pero le echaban la culpa a su papá de San Antonio. En papá platicaba que quizás Dios le dio poder a San Antonio de que sacara el difunto ese pa que dijiera quién lo había matao.

Llevó San Antonio a su papá pa aá tamién, que si quién había matao a ese hombre, y se levantó el difunto.

—Ese hombre no me ha matao; es un falso testimonio.

—Pos diga quién, quién lo mató.

—Eso no poo dijir yo.

Loo lo enterraron otra vez, pero salvó al papá de San Antonio. Por eso digo que San Antonio es muy milagroso.

Aquí en años pasaos cuando la nieve, andaba barriéndola yo paá y pacá. Perdí una bolsa de doscientos pesos ahi corriendo con el trator paá y pacá. Pasaron tres días. Anduvimos yo y mi hija mirando a ver si la jallábanos en las pilas de nieve que arrempujaba paá. No jallamos nada. ¡Nada!

Porque una mañana aquí le dije a la Mague,

—Voy a dijile a San Antoñito que me apronte mi bolsa con los doscientos pesos.

Pos salí. Aquí me di una vuelta pacá y loo me volví acá. Ya vide.

—Mira que cuadrito está aquí.

¡Quién sabe cuántos pasaron por arriba de ella! Yo con el trator y nada. Esa mañana me levanté, gracias a mi Dios y a San Antonio, porque le pidí a San Antoñito,

—Apróntame mi bolsa.

Dicho y hecho. Esa mañana me la aprontó. Es muy milagroso, San Antonio. No es la primer gaita que hace. He perdido bolsas ahi y las he jallao. Perdí una con trescientos pesos tamién y la jallé. De moo que San Antonio es muy milagroso. San Antonio es güena gente.

José B. Quintana

Saint Anthony is a Miracle Maker

There was a story going around that my dad used to tell about the fact that San Antonio is a miracle maker. An accusation was leveled against San Antonio's father. People buried the dead person, who had been murdered by another man, but they were blaming San Antonio's father for the murder. Dad used to say that perhaps God gave San Antonio power to exhume the dead person so that he could tell who had killed him.

San Antonio also took his father over there, to find out who had killed that man, and the dead person rose up.

"That man didn't kill me; it's false testimony."

"Well, say who did it, say who killed you."

"That I cannot say."

Then they buried him again, but he saved San Antonio's father. That is why I say that San Antonio is a miracle maker.

Here many years ago it snowed, and I was sweeping the snow this way and that way. I lost a wallet with $200 while going back and forth over the snow with the tractor. Three days went by. My daughter Margaret and I kept on looking to see if we could find it in the stacks of snow that I was piling up over in a certain direction. We didn't find anything. Nothing!

One morning I said to Margaret:

"I'm going to ask my little friend San Antoñito to find my wallet with the $200."

Well, I went outside. I went for a little stroll in this direction and then I turned back. Then I suddenly saw something.

"Look at this little square-like thing."

Who knows how many people stepped over it! Including me with the tractor, and finding nothing. That morning I got up, thanks to God and to San Antonio, because I asked my beloved friend San Antoñito, "Find my wallet for me."

No sooner said than done. That morning he found it just like that. He is a real miracle maker, San Antonio is. It's not the first time he's done so. I've lost wallets in the past and I've found them. I also lost one with $300 and I found it. And so San Antonio is a miracle maker. San Antonio is good people.

José B. Quintana

Martina L. Sánchez

MARTINA L. SÁNCHEZ

Nació: El 4 de marzo, 1908
Villanueva, NM
Entrevista: El 5 de agosto, 1992
Villanueva, NM

Born: March 4, 1908
Villanueva, NM
Interview: August 5, 1992
Villanueva, NM

Iban las brujas brincando

Decía mi agüelito que cuando él y otros iban paá pal Puerto de Luna isque ahi iban las brujas brincando adelante de ellos. Pero no podían saber quiénes eran. El que sí vido que era una mujer, jue mi tío Rumaldo, hermano de mamá. Ése sí sabía porque se casó con una mujer de allá de Puerto de Luna. Y iban en la tarde—iba casarse alguien allá—y cuando menos acordaron isque ahi iba una brasa delantito del carro de ellos. Pero no supieron quién era. Si luego tiene uno novias asina de más antes, isque se prontan, ¿no?

Mi tía Tanislada, una tía de los Flores estos que están aquí, platicaba que iba mi compadre Rumaldo pallá a la boda.

Y luego isque dijo mi tía Tanislada,

—Ahi va la novia de Rumaldo [las brasas]. (Risas) Ahi va la novia de antes de Rumaldo. A ver qué hace.

Mi tía Tanislada decía que era novia de antes de Rumaldo, pero no sé si sería o no sería. Pero decían que isque había munchas brujas.

Lo que sí me platicaba a mí mi tío Rumaldo era que sí había oido hablar desa Llorona. Era aá en San José. Mi esposo Simón me dijo. Isque ahi se mantenía en el río [el Río Pecos]. Tenían un puente las gentes, asegún él, y ahi estaba llora y llora nomás pasaban ellos pal otro lao, o par este lao. Ahi estaba llora y llora. Pero aquí en Villanueva no la oía yo.

Martina L. Sánchez

The Witches Were Jumping About

My grandpa used to say that when they were headed for Puerto de Luna that the witches would jump about in front of them. But they couldn't decide who they were. The one who did see that it was a woman was my Uncle Rumaldo, my mom's brother. He knew because he married a woman from over in Puerto de Luna. I understand they were traveling in the evening—someone was going to get married over there—and when they least expected it, there were sparks jumping about right in front of the wagon. But they didn't find out who it was. It so happens that once in a while old girlfriends might appear as witches at night, they say.

My Aunt Tanislada, an aunt of the Floreses who live here, used to say that her *compadre* Rumaldo was on his way to the wedding.

Then I understand that my Aunt Tanislada said:

"There goes Rumaldo's girlfriend [the sparks]. (Laughter.) There goes Rumaldo's old girlfriend. Let's see what she does now."

My Aunt Tanislada used to say that she was Rumaldo's old girlfriend, but I don't know if she was or not. Well, no more witches for me. Rumor has it that there were lots of them.

One thing my Uncle Rumaldo used to tell me is that he had heard about the Wailing Woman. That was over in San José. My husband Simón also told me. I understand that the Wailing Woman spent all of her time in the Pecos River. There was a bridge, according to my husband, and as soon as people crossed one way or the other, there she was, crying and crying. But not here, not here in Villanueva. I didn't hear her cry over here.

Martina L. Sánchez

Endalecio P. Sena

ENDALECIO P. SENA

Nació: El 7 de noviembre, 1922
Sena, NM
Entrevista: El 13 de julio, 1992
Sena, NM
Fallecido

ENDALECIO P. SENA
Born: November 7, 1922
Sena, NM
Interview: July 13, 1992
Sena, NM
Deceased

El ojo

Muncha gente no cree del mal ojo. Si una persona le hace ojo a una criatura, como ora una criatura chiquita, se enferma. Si se le hace muy bonita a usté y empieza ella a travesiar con usté y a rirse, y usté con ella, y le da gusto, antonces puede hacele ojo, ¿ve?

Si le hacía ojo usté a una criatura y salía del lugar—de su casa—donde estaba ella, le empezaba a doler la cabeza al muchito o la muchita. Antonces se muría si no le daba agua con el tiempo, pero tiene que buscar un Juan pa que le dé agua en la boca con su boca de él a la criatura.

A mí se me murió una muchita despés que salió güen y sana de aquí en casa [Sena]. Yo andaba en Santa Rita. Derechito al espital se jue. Y se le secaban los ojos.

Salimos día jueves de aquí. Pa día sábado se murió la muchita aá en Silver City en el espital. Y no le hallaron qué tenía los dotores. ¡Nada! Cuando íbanos ahi en Socorro, llore y llore y llore. Derechito al espital la llevé. Y allá se me murió.

Ése es l'ojo. Muncha gente dice que no es verdá. Pero sí, sí hacen mal ojo. Y no nomás a m'hijita. ¡A munchos!

Y otra cosa, tamién que usté acaricie una criatura muncho, le pega una tristeza. Como yo creo, dígase que estuvo m'hijo aquí en casa y lo acariciaba muncho, y si yo me voy lejos de aquí, se entristece de una manera que se va murir. ¿Ve?

Porque le pasó al difunto Polo Chávez. El chamaquito de él, el primero. Lo acariciaba muncho y lo traiba a caballo pa ondequiera con él y todo. Y él jue a trabajar a las minas a Ratón, solo, porque la Lola se quedó aquí en Sena. Tuvieron que trailo. Nomás lo trujieron y descansó el muchito, que toavía está vivo.

Es tristeza. Eh, echan menos a la persona y se entristezan y se mueren, de tristeza. ¡Sí señor!

Endalecio P. Sena

The Evil Eye

A lot of people don't believe in the evil eye. If one person casts an evil spell on another, if the evil eye is cast on a child, like a baby, let's say, it gets sick. If a child strikes you as very pretty and it begins to play around with you and to laugh, and you with the child, you derive pleasure from that, right? Then you cast the evil eye, got it? Because you admired someone too much [cast the evil eye].

And after you left the place where it was, the person [the baby] affected with the evil eye would begin to suffer a headache and the little baby would die if in due time it wasn't given water. Then you have to look for a Juan so he can give water with his own mouth to the baby.

I lost a little girl after leaving the house here in Sena in perfectly good health. I was in Santa Rita at the time. She went straight to the hospital. And her eyes were drying up.

We left Sena on a Thursday. By Saturday the little girl died in the hospital over in Silver City. And the doctors never could find out what was wrong with her. Nothing! When we were close to Socorro, she was crying and crying and crying. I took her straight to the hospital. And that's where she died.

That's the evil eye. A lot of people say that it's not true. But yes, it is true. And it's not only my daughter. It happens to many others!

And another thing, sadness can overcome a child if you are too affectionate with it. I believe, for example, that if my son came to visit me and I was very affectionate with him, and if I left to go far away from here, he would get sad in such a way that he'd die. You see?

Because that's what happened to the late Polo Chávez with his little boy, the first one. He used to be very affectionate with him and he took him on horseback everywhere he went and everything. And when he went to work at the mines in Raton, alone, because Lola stayed back here in Sena, they had to go after him. As soon as they brought him back, the little boy got well. By the way, he is still living.

That comes from sadness. Ah, a child misses someone and is overcome with sadness and dies from sadness. Yes sir!

Endalecio P. Sena

El dinero hace ruido

Pus le vo a decir una cosa. Aquí en Sena hubo un lugar. La casa era de mi papá, el dijunto Carmen Sena. Y hubo un lugar en que teníanos marranos. Teníanos como unos doce, trece marranos allí. Y estos marranos jociaban con la trompa y había un horno que se calentaba la gente con leña, puesto en un rincón, como ora semejancia aquí.

Y ahi onde tenían el piso, onde ponían la leña, ahi estaba un entierro. Ese entierro lo sacó mi tocayo, Turnino Sena, porque él se llamaba Endalecio Turnino, de donde vino mi nombre Endalecio. Y el dijunto Lucario Octavo que estaba en el entierro, sepa Dios que tanto sacaría. Sepa Dios. Pero sí era dinero. En oro, en oro.

Y después traiban oro ellos [los Octavo] de ahi y todo. Pero la viejita, la dijunta Gabina, vino y le avisó a en papá aquí, que había salido con una olla de barro, una olla de barro, de que teníanos pa los marranos. Y que la habían traido pacá, pa case mi tocayo Turnino. Y loo la viejita la llamaron pallá onde jalló la olla y le pagaron pero no les quiso entregar nada.

Hallamos el hoyo donde lo sacaba. Era un hoyo grandotote. Sepa Dios qué tanta cantidá de dinero sacarían. Pero era dinero en oro. El dijunto Juan Aguilar, el que crió a mi compadre Pablo, ése era el que tenía ese entierro, ¿ve?

Y luego no dejaba durmir el ruido allí en la casa onde hizo mi compadre Pablo. Nomás sacaron el entierro y se acabó el ruido. Se acabó el ruido. Porque el dinero, según estos viejitos, hace ruido cuando está enterrao. Yo creo que quiere que lo saque alguien y lo usen.

En aquellos años llovía muncho para las siembras, y había buenas cosechas. No había uso pal dinero. No había uso. El uso era nomás pa vistirse uno, y era total. ¡Lo demás qué! Y loo la ropa pus muy barata, ¿verdá? Muy barata. Pero dinero no había uso y la gente enterraba el dinero por la crencia, crencia del dinero, ¿ve?

El dijunto Francisco García dejó dinero enterrao que sepa Dios ónde. Lo han buscao por todo esto de aquí y no lo han podido hallar. ¿Me entiende? Pero el hijo dél, él sí sabía ónde estaba porque el viejito le notificó. El viejito no sabía contar. ¡No sabía nada! Y mi tocayo Turnino, él le contaba el dinero a él cuando agarraba

Endalecio P. Sena

Money Makes Noise

Well, I'm going to tell you something. There was a place here in Sena. The house belonged to my dad, the late Carmen Sena. And there was a place where we raised hogs. We had about 12, 13 hogs there. And these hogs would dig around with their snouts, and there was a beehive oven in a corner that people fed wood to where they got warm. Like the one here.

And there where they had the throw rug, where they put the wood, that's where a treasure was. My namesake, Turnino Sena, because his name was Endalecio Turnino, which is where my name came from, he dug up that buried treasure. And the late Lucario Octavo who was involved with the treasure, God knows how much money he took out. God knows. But it was money. It was gold, in gold coins.

And later on the Octavo family was hauling gold from there and everything. But the little old lady, the late Gabina, came here and informed my dad that she had found a clay pot, a clay pot like what the hogs ate from. And I understand that they had brought it here, to my namesake Turnino's house. And then they asked the little old lady to go over where she found the clay pot—and they paid her, but she refused to turn over anything from the treasure.

We found the hole where she was digging up money. It was a huge hole. God knows how much money she took out. But it was money in gold coins. The late Juan Aguilar, the one who raised my *compadre* Pablo, he's the one who had that treasure, you see?

And to top it off, because of the noise there in the house that my *compadre* Pablo built, you couldn't sleep. No sooner did they take out the treasure and that was the end of the noise. Because money, according to old-timers, makes noise when it's buried. I guess it's because the money wants somebody to dig it up and use it.

Back years ago, it rained a lot during planting season, so the crops were good. There was no use for money. There just wasn't any need for it. The only need for money was to buy clothes, and that was it. As for the rest, what for? And then clothing was very inexpensive, right? Very cheap. But money, there wasn't any need for it so these people would bury their money because that's what they believed in, that was the thing to do, you see?

The late Francisco García left money buried, but God knows

Endalecio P. Sena

pensión del gobierno. Cuando la guerra del Valverde que le llamaban. Sepa Dios cuándo sería. Pero él agarraba pensión por eso. Y se me hace que agarraba noventa y cuatro pesos al mes. Era un dineral bárbaro en esos tiempos. Y el viejito seguido andaban espiándolo a ver ónde escondía. Sepa Dios ónde lo escondería. Nunca lo hallaron.

Pero tenían la crencia de esconder dinero. No sé pa qué. Quizás pensaban que iban vivir por siglos y siglos. Sepa Dios.

¡Diablo sí hay!

Pues le vo a dicir una cosa. Mire. ¡Diablo sí hay! Sí hay, porque el diablo quiso ponerse en contra de la voluntá de Dios. Y le dio su reinao a él. Que ése es lo que está trujando orita, el diablo, ¿ve? Porque una persona que tiene fe en Dios no hay quién lo moleste. Porque Dios dice asina, "Mientras tú tengas fe en Mí, no hay persona en el mundo que se meta contigo."

Y mire. L'agüelo, ésas son cosas que tenían los viejitos pa metele miedo a uno. Había temor. La Llorona, todo ese negocio, ¿ve?

Aquí había un hombre que se llamaba Patricio García. Andaba metiéndole miedo a la plebe, a la plebe grande, como José Hilario, mi compadre Pablo y ésos. Le metieron una pedrada y desmayaron al agüelo. Y él, ya estaba más y más abusadito. Y nojotros todos los chiquitos nos juimos pacá pa la casa. Y José Hilario le dio una pedrada a en primo Patricio que, que lo desmayó.

Y de ahi se quitaron los agüelos. ¿Sabe cómo? No hay brujería si usté tiene fe en Dios; no puede hacele naiden nada. No importa quién. Puede rascarse o sea lo que sea, no pueden hacele nada. Porque la fe en Dios es la que cuenta.

Endalecio P. Sena

where he left it. People have looked for it all around here and they haven't been able to find it. You understand? But his son, he knew where it was because the old man told him. The old man didn't know how to count. He didn't know anything! And my namesake Turnino, he's the one who used to count the money for him whenever he used to receive a pension check from the government. This was when the Valverde War took place. God knows when that was. But that's why he received a pension. And I believe that he used to get $94 a month. It was a whole lot of money back in those days. And people were constantly spying on the little old man to see where he buried the money. God knows where he might have buried it. Nobody ever found it.

But people were in the habit of hiding their money. I don't know why. I guess they thought they were going to live forever and ever. God knows why.

There is a Devil!

I'm going to tell you something. There is a devil! There is, because it's the devil who tried to go against God's will. And God gave him his kingdom. That's what is making noises now, the devil, you see? Because for a person who has faith in God, there's no one who can bother him. Because God says the following: "As long as you have faith in Me, there's not a person in the world who will mess around with you."

As for the bogeyman, those were things the old-timers did to scare us with. There was fear. The Wailing Woman and all that business, you see?

There was a man here whose name was Patricio García. He went around scaring children, the older ones, like José Hilario, my *compadre* Pablo, and those guys. They smacked him with a rock and knocked him out cold. He was getting wiser and wiser. All the rest of us children, we just went home. And José Hilario smacked cousin Patricio with a rock to the point of knocking him out.

From then on there were no more bogeymen. You know how that happened? There's no witchcraft if you have faith in God; no one can cause you harm. It doesn't matter who it is. You can scratch your head or whatever, they can't do anything to you. It's faith in God that counts.

Endalecio P. Sena

Nicolás Padilla and Nobertita Tafoya y Padilla

NOBERTITA TAFOYA Y PADILLA

Nació: El 6 de junio, 1920
San Ysidro (Norte), NM
Entrevista: El 22 de octubre, 1992
Ancón, NM

Born: June 6, 1920
San Ysidro (Norte), NM
Interview: October 22, 1992
Ancón, NM

Perdió los ojos

Pues hay gentes que les hacen ojo a los *babies*, porque ya a una hermanita mía le hicieron ojo y no la curaron, y se hizo ciega. Perdió los ojos y se murió. Tenía tres años. Y eso dijieron que era, ojo.

Dicen que cuando ya se pasa un viernes, ya no descansa. Ya ella se había pasao un viernes. Ya no. Ella duró como dos años, yo creo.

A la otra hermanita le pasó la misma cosa tamién. Nomás que ella tenía más que un año. Estaba *baby*. Tamién le pasó eso. Yo no sé. Yo creo que la misma cosa le pasó porque tamién se le cosieron los ojos, como cosidos.

Parecía que le habían echao agua jirviendo pa dentro. Y no miraba. Y eso dijieron que era del mal ojo. Pero no se supo quién lo hizo.

Se aprontaba el diablo

Mi agüelita me platicaba a mí de cómo se aprontaba el diablo. Una noche habían ido ella y unas amigas al baile, y se había aprontao una cosa de ésas que se hizo esplosión. Se apagó la sala y se quedó apestando. Se quedaron a oscuras. Salieron todos pa juera, decía ella, no sé. Que había entrao un hombre con vestido y ése esploró y dejó toda jedionda la sala. Se salieron todos. Ya no quisieron ir pa dentro. Ya se acabó el baile. Ya no siguió aprontándose eso. Yo no sé por qué.

Y por eso me daba miedo a mí ir a los bailes. Pero nunca vide nada yo. Yo me acuerdo de eso, de las brujerías. Yo creo que sí tenían valores de andar haciendo mal.

Nosotros teníanos un tío enfermo. Cerquita de nojotros vivía y ese hombre estaba embrujao. Venían estas brasas y subían la cama y loo primero llegaba ese tecolote y gruñía en el chiflón de la estufa. Ya cuando ese tecolote llegaba ya mi tío estaba

Nobertita Tafoya y Padilla

She Lost Her Eyesight

There are those people who can cast an evil eye on babies, because that happened to a sister of mine, and they couldn't cure her, so she went blind. She lost her eyesight and died. She was three years old. And that's what people said it was, the evil eye.

It is said that once the evil eye goes past a Friday, the chances of the child getting well are hopeless. She had already gone past a Friday. There was no hope. She lasted about two years, I believe.

The same thing happened to my other little sister. The only thing is that she was already over a year old. She was still a baby. The same thing happened to her. I can't explain it. I guess the same thing happened because her eyes were closed shut, like they were sewn together.

It looked as though they had poured boiling water in her eyes. And she couldn't see a thing. And that, people used to say, was a result of the evil eye. But no one ever found out who it was who did it.

The Devil Would Suddenly Appear

My grandma used to tell me about how the devil would appear. One night she and some women friends had gone to a dance, and one of those objects appeared and it exploded. The dance hall turned dark and it began to stink. Everybody was left in the dark. Everyone left the dance hall, or so she said, I don't know. Rumor has it that a man in a suit had entered and exploded something and left the dance hall, stinking to high heaven. Everybody ran out. They refused to go back in. The dance simply ended. And that object never showed up again. I don't know why not.

And that's why I was afraid to go to dances. But I never saw anything myself. I do remember about witchlike things. I guess they did have evil intentions of going around causing harm.

There was an uncle of ours who was ill. He lived quite close to us and that man was bewitched. These sparks would show up and they'd climb on top of the bed and then an owl would show up first

Nobertita Tafoya y Padilla

muriéndose. Parecía que ya se iba morir; ya no se movía ni nada. Y luego comenzaban las brasas otra vez. Ya que se iba el tecolote, empezaban las brasas tras y tras, y nojotros con miedo. Estábanos medianos. Y iba mi tío, otro tío, a espiar ese tecolote pa ver si lo mataba. Nunca pudo matalo; nunca pudo matalo. Y al fin se murió mi tío.

Pero bien, como muerto lo ibas a ver tú, cuando estaba el tecolote ahi y la mujer de él, mi tía, tenía muncho miedo porque sonaba el chiflón de la estufa como un buho. Muy feo. Eso sí vide yo.

Puede que tuivera yo unos catorce años, quince por ahi. De San Ysidro era mi tío. Salían las brasas del suelo. Hacían asina y loo se movían parriba. Parriba de la casa. Ahi andaban, bien feo.

Mi tío vino de un lugar que estaba trabajando y de allá vino enfermo, que allá le hicieron el mal. No sé yo por qué. Ya no descansó. Jue a uno de ésos que curan, arbularios, pero no descansó.

Pero decían más antes que sí se aprontaban munchas cosas. Salían lloronas de una cueva que está aá en San Ysidro como en un peñasco asina, pero yo nunca oí ni las vide yo.

174

Creo que era un dijunto que andaba penando, porque ya no se golvió a ver. Ya yo tengo aquí en Ancón cincuenta y tres años, y no ha oido decir más.

Nobertita Tafoya y Padilla

and make an irritable noise on the stove's chimney. By the time that owl showed up, my uncle was already dying. It seemed as though he was going to die; he could no longer move or anything. And then, there would go the sparks once again. Then the owl would take off, and the sparks started popping and popping, and there we were, scared to death. We were young. And an uncle of mine, another uncle, would go spy on the owl to see if he could kill it. He was never able to kill it; he never could. Finally my uncle passed away.

But fine, even when you saw him lying there as if he were dead, when the owl was there, and his wife, that is, my aunt, she was very afraid because the stove chimney was making noises like an owl. It was very strange. That I did see myself.

I must have been about 14 or 15. My uncle was from San Ysidro. The sparks would come out from the floor. They'd move like so and then they'd shoot up. They'd shoot up above the house. There they'd be, hovering about; it was quite ugly.

My uncle came from a place where he was working, where he had already gotten sick, for it was there that they cast an evil spell on him. I don't know why. He never got well again. He went to one of those herbalists who can cure you, but he didn't get well.

But people long ago used to say that yes, many things would appear. Wailing women would come out from a cave, like a large rock, that's over in San Ysidro, but I never heard any more about it, nor did I see those things.

I believe it was a dead person who was grieving, because it was never seen again. As for me, I've already been here in Ancón 53 years, and I haven't heard anything else about it.

Nobertita Tafoya y Padilla

Viviana Tapia

VIVIANA TAPIA

Nació: El 23 de febrero, 1908
La Sierra, NM
Entrevista: El 13 de febrero, 1993
Ribera, NM

Born: February 23, 1908
La Sierra, NM
Interview: February 13, 1993
Ribera, NM

A m'hija le hicieron ojo

A m'hija le hicieron ojo. Y lo tiene gacho toavía su ojo. Que andaba como de reina ella cuando le hicieron ojo.

Y munchos asina le[s] hacen ojo y no creen en eso, pero sí hay. Sí les hacen ojo. Y se han muerto munchos del ojo que les hacen. Si no los curan antes del viernes, se mueren. Algunos que les hacen ojo en la sangre, ¿no? Se les queda asina. Y se van quedando mal.

Pero los que les hacen en la jiel, se les revienta la jiel y se mueren. Se mueren con el ojo porque se revientan adentro, ¿ve? ¡Diuna vez! Con el ojo, no creen eso, pero sí es. Y algunos les hacen más mal. Como le digo que en la sangre no, porque se despierta la cosa. Pero en la jiel les hacen ojo; se les revienta la jiel. Se gomitan y se mueren. Ya no hay remedio. Taa los que les hacen en la sangre pus los curan antes de que se llegue el viernes y descansan. Y del otro modo no.

Pus a mi hija ella andaba de reina. Andaba en la iglesia. Traiba corona y estaba muy bonita. Le hicieron ojo. Y el ojo se le ladió. Y el ojo lo tiene gacho todavía. Ése no se le enderezó. Porque era muy bonita le hicieron ojo.

Lo curaban con remedios. Lo escupía con caña aigra con cachana. Tenían que escupila—escupiles la cara con ella pa que se les quite, que se les quitara. Es cachana, una medecina que se llamaba cachana. Y ésa la mascaban los mismos que la escupían. Y tenía que ser un Juan o una Juana pa que lo curara, ¿ve? Porque de otro modo no. Tenía que ser eso. Si no, no.

Siempre más antes cuando uno vía un niño que estaba bonito tenía que hacele una cruz en la frente pa no hacele ojo al niño o a la niña, lo que sea. Ya cuando están más grandes pus cuando acuerda uno les hacen el ojo, como le digo que le hicieron a mi hija. Y asina la curamos, menos el ojo gacho, pero escupiéndole la cara un Juan sanó. De otro modo no, no se puede.

Viviana Tapia

My Daughter Got the Evil Eye

My daughter got the evil eye, and she still has a droopy eye. She was the reigning queen when someone cast the evil eye on her.

Many people suffer the same fate, and they don't believe in that sort of thing, but it is true. People do suffer from the evil eye. Many people have died from it. If those who are afflicted with it are not treated before the first Friday after the spell, they'll die. Some are afflicted in the bloodstream, right? And it stays there. There they are, suffering.

But those who are afflicted in the bile [liver], it will burst and they die. They die from the evil eye because the bile will spread inside the body, you understand? Right away! All because of the evil eye; people don't believe in that, but it does happen. And some people are hit harder than others. For example, in the bloodstream, as I say, but in the bile [liver] if the evil eye is cast, the bile ruptures. People vomit and die. There's no cure for it. At least those who are affected in the bloodstream, they can be treated and cured before the next Friday rolls around. Otherwise, there's no hope.

Well, my daughter was acting as queen as part of the church celebrations and activities. She was wearing a crown and looked very pretty. Then someone hit her with the evil eye and she became ill. And her eye tilted to one side. She still has a droopy eye. It didn't straighten out. They did it because she was very pretty.

People used to treat the evil eye with remedies. For example, you treated it by spitting wild pie plant with *cachana*, a root used to ward off evil. You had to spit it—spit in the face of the afflicted so that the evil eye could be lifted, so that it would go away. It's *cachana*, that's what the medicine is called. The same persons who would spit it are the ones who would chew it (the root). And it had to be a Juan or a Juana in order to cure the victim, got it? Any other way was not possible. It had to be one or the other in order for them to cure the afflicted. If not, nothing doing.

In the past whenever you saw a pretty child, you had to make the sign of the cross on its forehead so as not to inflict it with the evil eye, whether it was a baby boy or a baby girl. Later on as they get older, when you least expect it, they're afflicted with the evil eye, like what happened to my daughter. And that's the way we cured her, except for the droopy eye, by having a Juan spit on her face. Any other way, it's useless.

Viviana Tapia

Me habían hecho mal en el durazno

A mí me hicieron un mal, y no supe yo cómo. Me dijieron que me habían hecho mal en el durazno que sequé. Sequé durazno, lo colgué en la percha, y ahi jue onde me hicieron el mal. No me dejaban hablar. No podía hablar. Y jui a una médica a que me curara. Dijo que me habían hecho mal en el durazno. Me dio medecinas. Me curó y sané. Y me dijo que la mujer que me había hecho mal iba a volver a mi casa, pero nunca volvió. Y yo la conocía a ella. Era del mismo lugar aá en San Juan. Yo no sé por qué mi hizo mal.

Por mal idea, yo creo, por eso le hacen a uno mal, por la mal idea que le tienen a uno, o la envidia que le tienen a uno, pa tener fregao a uno. ¿Ve? De modo que es la que reina hoy en día. Por la mal idea.

Y me dijo la médica,

—No vayas a volver a comer durazno. Lo apeas de la percha y lo echas en la lumbre.

Tuve que quemalo. No volví a comer más durazno de ése seco, ¿no? Lo arranqué de la percha y lo quemé, porque ella me dijo que lo quemara.

No sé qué le pondría la mujer de San Juan al durazno. No sé cuándo tampoco. Sería punto de noche o cuando no estaba en casa yo. No sé pero en el durazno hizo el mal.

Ya la que me hizo el mal ya hasta se murió. No era más de vecina de allá. No era más de vecina, porque le agarré yo mala pica. Yo no sé pero dicían que era de las muy güenas pa hacer mal. Era muy güena. ¡De veras!

Y mi hija no cree en eso, pero sí hay gente asina. Yo les digo que sí.

Viviana Tapia

Someone Had Bewitched My Peaches

Someone bewitched me, and I never found out how. I was told that someone had bewitched the peaches I dried. I sundried peaches, I hung them on the clothesline, and that's how I was bewitched. I wasn't allowed to talk. I couldn't talk. So I went to a folk practitioner so she could cure me. She said that someone had put a curse on my peaches. She recommended several remedies. She treated me and I got well. And she told me that the woman who had bewitched me would be returning to my house, but she never did. And I knew her. She was from the same place I was from, over in San Juan. I don't know why she did it. To cause me harm, I guess.

Some people bewitch you because they have it in for you, or because they're jealous of you, so they can have you all screwed up, you understand? That's the kind of thing that's going on nowadays, just because someone bears ill will toward you.

So the folk practitioner said to me:

"Don't go eat any more of those dried peaches. You take them down from the clothesline and you toss them in the fire."

I had to burn them all. I didn't eat any of them anymore. I yanked them off the clothesline and I burned them as I was told.

I don't know what the lady from San Juan put in the peaches. I don't know when she did it, either. Maybe it happened at night or when I wasn't home. I just don't know, but the evil was in the peaches.

The lady who bewitched me, she's already dead. She was barely a neighbor, and I developed a bad taste in my mouth for her. I don't know, but people say that she was one of the very good ones at what evil people do. She was really good at it. Really!

My daughter doesn't believe in that sort of thing, but people like that lady do exist. I tell people that it's so.

Viviana Tapia

Carmel Ulibarrí

CARMEL ULIBARRÍ

Nació: El 27 de noviembre, 1920
El Barranco, NM
Entrevista: El 22 de agosto, 1989
El Barranco, NM

Born: November 27, 1920
El Barranco, NM
Interview: August 22, 1989
El Barranco, NM

Le vido los cuernos y la cola

Éste era un hombre que iba caminando a pie y era muy borracho y muy mal portao. Iba caminando y loo es que se le aprontó un hombre muy grande en un caballo negro. Y es que le dijo,

—¿Par ónde vas? ¿Quieres irte conmigo? Yo te llevo. Vamos a un baile muy grande.

Y el hombre a pie pensó irse con él. Se iba a subir y loo es que le dio miedo. Es que le dijo,

—No. Tú eres un hombre muy estraño.

Porque es que el hombre a pie le vido los cuernos y la cola. Loo le puso las cruces. Al momento pegó un traquido y olió puro azufre y se despareció el caballo y el hombre. Era la cosa mala, ¿ves? Y la traiba él.

Te va llevar el diablo

Mis agüelitos, mis tíos, y toos me contaban historias. Ya me acuerdo de muy pocas, pero me acuerdo. Cuando nos dijían del diablo, nos dijían,

—Si haces un mal te va llevar el diablo—.

Y luego, pus, uno tenía miedo, ves, y ya no hacía aquel mal. Se precuraba uno de detenerse lo mejor que se podía, porque uno tenía miedo que sí se lo juera a llevar el diablo.

El cuento es que en las noches, ya cuando cerraba la noche, le daban de cenar a uno y le dijían, si empezaba uno a brincotiar y a saltar,

—Va venir l'agüelo—o—Va venir la Llorona—.

Pus, no, siempre siguimos. Ya vinían y tocaban la puerta. Se asomaba uno. Vía uno una cosa muy fiera y ésa era la Llorona. Pus tenía uno miedo. Pronto rompía uno corriendo. Abajo de la camalta iba a dar uno. De abajo de la camalta tenían que sacarnos dormidos en veces porque nos daba miedo. Teníanos miedo.

Nomás nos dijían los padres que si éranos malcriaos nos iba a salir la cosa mala. Eso es lo único que nos dijían nomás.

Carmel Ulibarrí

He Saw that He Had Horns and a Tail

This is about a man who was walking and was very drunk a lot and behaved very badly. He was walking along and the story has it that a very large man popped in front of him on a black horse. Rumor has it that the large man said to him:

"Where are you going? Do you want to come with me? I'll take you along. We're going to a big dance."

And the man on foot decided to take off with him. He was about to hop on the horse, when he suddenly got scared. He said to him:

"No. You're a very strange man."

I understand that the man on foot saw that the one on horseback had horns and a tail. Then he made the sign of the cross [to ward off evil]. At that very moment the man on horseback made a cracking sound. He reeked of pure sulphur, and both the horse and the man disappeared. It was an evil spirit, you see? And that man was possessed with it.

The Devil's Going to Take You Away

My grandparents, my uncles, and everybody used to tell me stories. I remember very few, but I remember some. When they used to tell us about the devil, they'd say, "If you do anything bad the devil's going to take you away." And then, well, you got scared, you see, and so you didn't do whatever bad thing you had in mind. You did your best to hold back the best way you could, because you were afraid that the devil would take you away.

The fact is that at night, when it was already dark, they'd feed you supper and they'd warn you that if you started cutting up and jumping around, "The bogeyman is going to come" or "The Wailing Woman is coming." We'd keep messing around anyway. Then someone would come and knock at the door. We'd take a peek. We'd see a very ugly thing, and it was the Wailing Woman. Why of course you got scared. You'd dash off running and get right under the bed. Once in a while they'd have to take us out from underneath the bed where we'd fallen asleep after being scared out of our wits. We were afraid.

Our parents used to tell us that if we misbehaved, an evil thing was going to come after us.

Carmel Ulibarrí

Un lugar encantao

Cuando está un lugar encantao asina dicen que hay dinero. Hay dinero. Más antes enterraba la gente el dinero en cueros de animales. Mataban los animales y loo vinían y guardaban el dinero ahi, en los cueros. Los enterraban. De ahi no se hacían nada los cueros o el dinero. No se podrían.

Más antes no había más banco que onde enterraban el dinero y no lo enterraban en su casa. Iban y lo enterraban en los montes pa estar más seguros, pero se olvidaban ónde lo había enterrao. Ahi se quedaba el dinero hasta que otro lo jallaba. Ya cuando empezó a entrar la gente más viva, que traiban máquinas, pus ahi jallaron todo. Jallaban hasta desas joyas de oro tamién.

Yo me acuerdo que mi agüelo dijía que jallaban joyas de oro, llenas desas. No eran piedras. Eran como unos daimes, más chiquitos que el daime, pus ése era el dinero de antes.

Si hay tesoro, cuando hay dinero, se ve como una lucecita de noche donde está enterrao el dinero. Eso pasó con los cueros.

Carmel Ulibarrí

An Enchanted Place

Wherever there's an enchanted place, people claim that that's where there's money buried. A long time ago people slaughtered animals and they'd wrap up any money they had and bury it in animal hides. They'd bury them because nothing would happen to the hides (or the money). They wouldn't rot.

A long time ago there were no banks, but people wouldn't bury the money at home. They'd go and bury it in the mountains for safekeeping, but they would forget where it was buried. That's where the money stayed until somebody else found it. When wiser people started coming around, those who had machines, well, that's how they dug everything. Why, they even found those jewels made of gold also.

I remember my grandpa saying that people would find jewels made of gold. They weren't rocks. They were coins like dimes, a little smaller than a dime since that was the money in circulation back then.

If there's a buried treasure, one can see a little light at night where money is buried. That's what happened with the cowhides.

187

Carmel Ulibarrí

Crisóstomo Vigil

CRISÓSTOMO VIGIL

Nació: El 19 de junio, 1917
El Cerrito, NM
Entrevista: El 15 de julio, 1993
Villanueva, NM

Born: June 19, 1917
El Cerrito, NM
Interview: July 15, 1993
Villanueva, NM

189

Un león

Aquí en El Cerrito había un hombre, Luis Aragón. Ése te podía hacer dormir a ti con sus historias, y loo amanecía echándote chistes. Y aquí en Villanueva había varios también. Había lugares onde deshojaban maiz, unas pilas de maiz grandes. ¡Oh, muncho maiz! Y ahi se juntaba toda la gente. Pos yo llegué a ver este hombre; se sentaba en un lugar a echar chistes y a platicar historias. Hacía un trabajo muy grande. Y él nomás le pagaban pa que él estuviera allí echando historias.

Pero había cuentos que estos hombres tenían muy interesantes, unas historias muy curiosas. Me acuerdo de este hombre, Luis Aragón, que dicía que iba una vez pal lugar de las borregas. Ahi iba a un campamento y isque le había salido un león, muy malo, y les dijo a la gente,

—Pues saben ustedes que este león se me vino encima y abrió la boca, y yo que le metí la mano y lo agarré de la cola y le puché pallá asina y lo voltié al revés. (Risas).

¡Mentiras! Eran puras historias, pero tenía gracia pa dicilas, ¿ves? Y la gente se entretenía porque había munchas historias que sacaban d'estos hombres y no tenían fin. Puro dicir una y otra—de reyes, de mujeres, de lugares encantados.

Crisóstomo Vigil

A Lion

*H*ere at El Cerrito there was a man, Luis Aragón. That man was capable of putting you to sleep with his stories, and then he'd wake you up telling you jokes. And there were several like him here in Villanueva. There were places where they shucked corn, huge piles of corn. Oh, a lot of corn! And that's where all the people gathered. Well, I got to see this man; he'd sit down anywhere just to tell jokes and to tell stories. He did a great job. All people had to do was to pay him and there he'd be, telling you stories.

There were stories of course that these men told that were very interesting, some rather funny ones. I remember Luis Aragón used to tell the story about being on his way to a place where they herded sheep. He was headed for a campsite when I understand a very mean lion sneaked up on him. Then he told them (the people):

"Do you know that this lion jumped on top of me and it opened its mouth, and I stuck my hand in his mouth and I grabbed it by the tail and I pushed it like so and I turned him inside out?" (Laughter).

Lies! They were nothing but make-believe stories, but he had a funny way of telling them, you see. And people passed the time because there were lots of stories that they were able to get this man to tell them, and there was no end to them. It was a matter of saying one right after the other—about kings, about women, and about enchanted places.

Crisóstomo Vigil

El lugar estaba encantao

*H*abía un cuento de un rey lépero que tenía un lugar de encantamiento, y mantenía toda la gente encerrada. Luego este muchacho vino y les dijo a la gente que pa descantar ese lugar, tenían que hacer ciertas cosas. En el río, ya no corría l'agua. El lugar estaba encantao y la gente estaba prisionera, y esas dos cosas eran terribles.

El cuento es que este rey y los otros reyes se juntaban, y este muchacho se jue y se metió en un trozo de hueco de árbol. Ahi se juntaban los reyes estos a discutir.

—El río no corre porque tienen que dale una misa y una celebración a la Virgen, la Grandota. Y haciendo eso, corre el río. Y la hija del otro rey no sana si no hacen cierta cosa, y luego el encanto de la gente no sale si no hace cierta cosa.

Pus este muchacho oyó todo y vino y agarró su boguecito y un veliz y se jue y le dijo a la gente [del pueblito] que le hicieran una misa a la Grandota, a la Virgen, y luego corría el río. Y luego que hicieran este velorio pa quitar el encanto de la gente esa que tenían encantada y prisionera. Hicieron eso y soltaron la gente. Y loo pa que sanara la hija del rey este que la tenía sumetida otro rey, que tamién la encantó, que pusiera dinero la gente.

Pues a todos les cobró el muchacho, porque él agarró el secreto, ¿sabes? Pues es que supo su hermano dél y le dijo,

—Yo voy pallá a ver qué dicen los grandotes.

Se metió adentro del trozo del árbol después que le dijo a su hermano:

—Pus ora voy yo y escucho otra vez y voy y me hago rico tamién.

El cuento es que ahi onde estaban platicando los reyes, jue el único lugar onde los hermanos descubrieron los secretos.

—A mí se me hace que aquí en este trozo, hay escuchones— dijo uno de los reyes.

Se metió uno por un lao y otro por el otro, y loo vio otro rey un ajuero, onde se paró otro rey, y ahi lo pescaron al muchacho. Le dieron una garrotera y le mocharon la lengua pa que no anduviera de boquifloja. Era el hermano del otro que había oido todos estos

Crisóstomo Vigil

The Place Was Enchanted

*T*here was a story about a disreputable king who had an enchanted place where he kept all of the people locked up. Then this boy came and told the people that in order to disenchant the place, they had to do certain things. In the river, the water no longer ran. The place was enchanted and the people were prisoners, and both those things were terrible.

The story goes that this particular king and the other kings would get together, and this boy went and hid in a hollow tree trunk near where these kings would gather to discuss things. "The river doesn't run because they have to offer a mass and a celebration to the Virgin Mary. And if they do that, the river will start running. Another king's daughter won't get well unless they do a certain thing, and also the enchantment of the people cannot be lifted unless they do a certain thing."

Well, this boy heard everything and he went and got his horse carriage and a suitcase and took off to tell the people to offer a mass to the Great One, the Virgin Mary, and the river would then start running again. Then for them to say a *velorio* so as to lift the enchantment from those people who were prisoners and under that spell. That's what they did, and the people were set free. And then in order for this king's daughter to get well, because another king had subjected her to the same enchantment, the people had to donate money.

Well, the boy collected money from everyone, because he knew the secret, you see? Well, his brother supposedly found out and he said to him:

"I'm going over there to see what the big chiefs have to say."

He got inside the same hollow tree trunk after telling his brother:

"Well, now it's my turn to go listen, and I'm going to get rich as well."

The fact is that the place where the kings were conversing is the only place where the brothers could have found out about the secrets.

"It seems to me that in this tree trunk here, there's someone with huge ears," said one of the kings.

Crisóstomo Vigil

Adelaida Vigil

secretos, pero corrió el río. Se desencantó el lugar, como dice el cuento, y tamién sanó la hija del rey.

Todo era pa hacer un ejemplo del muchacho. Eran atroz los viejitos pero se pasaban el tiempo platicando historias y todo pero tamién caiban a un ejemplo de la vida. Como me dicía mi papá a mí,

—Sabes que vale más ser honesto y responsable porque todas las cosas del mundo que hace uno, güenas obras o malas, se las lleva el diablo, y las malas se las lleva con mucho más amor.

Mi papá me daba munchos ejemplos asina.

Crisóstomo Vigil

One king went in one end and another through the other side, and then another king saw another hole, which is where another king was standing, and that's where they caught the boy. They beat the pulp out of him and cut out his tongue so he wouldn't go around telling secrets. It was the brother of the one who had heard all of the secrets, but the river started running again just the same. The place became disenchanted, as the story goes, and the king's daughter got well also.

It was all to make an example of him. The old-timers were harsh, but the stories they passed the time of day telling ended with a moral about life. As my father used to say to me:

"You know that it's better to be honest and responsible because everything one does in life, whether good or bad deeds, the devil takes them with him, especially the evil ones, which he carries with all the love possible."

My father used to set many examples for me.

Crisóstomo Vigil

Summer Fiestas in Villanueva.

GLOSSARY

Regional	Standard

A

Regional	Standard
aá	allá
abrile	abrirle
abujas	agujas
abujero	agujero
abusadito	astuto
abusao	abusado
acabao	acabado
agarrao	agarrado
agüelita/o	abuelita/o
agüela/o	abuela/o
ahijao	ahijado
ahi	ahí
aigra	agria
aigre	aire
ajuera	afuera
ajuero	agujero
ajuir	huir
alabao	alabado
alborlario	herbolario
albulario	herbolario
algolavia	herbolaria
almuada	almohada
anancas	en ancas
andábanos	andábamos
anducio	vagamundo
antonces	entonces

Regional	Standard
apiarse	apearse
apalancao	apalancado
apió	apeó
aprontao	aprontado; aparecido
aprontó	apareció
arededores	alrededores
arrempujaba	empujaba
asegún	según
arrevisó	revisó
asina	así
azotalo	azotarlo

B

Regional	Standard
basuderos	basureros
bebito	niño
bisagüelo	bisabuelo
bonche	montón
brasas	fuegos fatuos
brincotiar	brincar
buscala	buscarla
buscao	buscado

C

Regional	Standard
cabándose	acabándose
cae	caer

Regional	Standard	Regional	Standard
caiban	caían	dejao	dejado
caidría	caería	dél	de él
calientitos	calentitos	delantito	en frente de
callí	caí	della	de ella
camalta	cama	dellos	de ellos
cantidá	cantidad	demasiao	demasiado
carpintiaba	carpinteaba	demen	denme
carpintiando	carpinteando	d'en	de en
cequia	acequia	den cuando	de vez en cuando
cerquías	cercanías	desas	de esas
chamaco	muchacho	descubrido	descubierto
chequiamos	vimos; revisamos	dese	de ese
chilito de perro	arzuelo	desiún	desde un
churrionela	chirrionera	deso	de eso
cimente	cemento	deste	de este
Colorao	Colorado	destendió	extendió
conetó	conectó	dicía/n	decía/n
confiao	confiado	dicilas	decirlas
contoy	con todo y	dicile	decirle
correla	correrla	dicir	decir
corríanos	corríamos	dicirte	decirte
coyonturas	coyunturas	dijían	decían
creiba/n	creía/n	dijíanos	decíamos
crencia	creencia	dijiendo	diciendo
creyen	creen	dijieron	dijeron
creyo	creo	dijile	decirle
crían	creían	dijir	decir
crivis	grieta	dijunta/o	difunta/o
cuidao	cuidado	dionde	donde
cuñao	cuñado	diondequiera	dondequiera
		dioquis	gratis

D

Regional	Standard	Regional	Standard
		diún	de un
		diuna	de una
daimes	diez centavos	diuna vez	de una vez
dale/s	darle/s	dotor	doctor
dao	dado	durmiría	dormiría

Regional	Standard	Regional	Standard
E		estaa	estaba
		estaan	estaban
ea	ella	estáanos	estábamos
echale	echarle	estábanos	estábamos
echao	echado	estao	estado
edá	edad	estógamo	estómago
embolao	emborrachado	estraño	extraño
embrujao	embrujado	estrito	estricto
empresto	presto		
enbrujaban	embrujaban	**F**	
enbrujao	embrujado		
enbrujaron	embrujaron	fascinaos	fascinados
enché	hinché	feya	fea
endiablao	endiablado	fieras	feas
enfermao	enfermado	fierros	hierros
enpaca	empaca	fiestín	festín
en papá	mi papá	folórafos	fonógrafos
ensayes	ensayos	fregao	fregado
enseñales	enseñarles	fundea	funde; destruye
enterrao	enterrado		
entrao	entrado	**G**	
entristezan	entristecen		
en veces	a veces	ganao	ganado
éranos	éramos	garrar	agarrar
escarbao	escarbado	golver	volver
escupiles	escupirles	golví	volví
escusao	excusado	golvía	volvía
ése	eso	golvieron	volvieron
espacharon	despacharon	golvió	volvió
esparciando	esparciendo	gomitan	vomitan
esperencia	experiencia	güelta	vuelta
espirituista	espiritualista;	güelven	vuelven
	espiritista	güen	buen
espital	hospital	güeno	bueno
esploró	exploró; explotó	güerta	huerta
esplosión	explosión	güey/es	buey/es

199

Regional	Standard	Regional	Standard
		jiel	hiel
H		jirviendo	hirviendo
		jociaban	hocicaban
ha	he	jondió	escarbó; tiró
hacele	hacerle	jue	fue
hacelos	hacerlos	juellas	huellas
hacíanos	hacíamos	juera	fuera
haiga	haya	juéranos	fuéramos
hicites	hiciste	jueron	fueron
hincaos	hincados	juerte	fuerte
historia	cuento	jugábanos	jugábamos
hogao	ahogado	jui	fui
hogó	ahogó	juila	brinco
		juimos	fuimos
I		juir	huir
		junta de	junto a; cerca de
íbanos	íbamos	juntábanos	juntábamos
ila	irla	juntra	junto a
intencionao	intencionado	juyendo	huyendo
isque	es que; dizque		
iyendo	yendo	**K**	
J		**L**	
jalaban	halaban	l'agarraba	la agarraba
jalar	halar	l'agua	el agua
jallaa	hallaba	l'alma	el alma
jallaba	hallaba	l'agüelo	el abuelo
jallábanos	hallábamos	l'abujero	el agujero
jallamos	hallamos	l'azogue	el azogue
jallao	hallado	l'empacho	el empacho
jallaron	hallaron	l'espinazo	la espalda
jallas	hallas	l'hospital	el hospital
jallo	hallo	l'ojo	el ojo
jalló	halló	l'orilla	la orilla
jedionda	hedionda	l'otra	la otra

Regional	Standard	Regional	Standard
ladió	ladeó	metelo	meterlo
lambió	lameó	m'hija	mi hija
lao/s	lado/s	m'hijo	mi hijo
lastimala	lastimarla	moo	modo
lastimao	lastimado	morao	morado
lego	luego	movíanos	movíamos
ler	leer	muchichito	muchachito
leyo	leo	muchito	muchachito
ligao	ligado	mujerero	mujeriego
liones	leones	muncha/o	mucha/o
llegábanos	llegábamos	murería	moriría
llegao	llegado	muría	moría
llenao	llenado	murir	morir
logo	luego	murre	muy
loo	luego		
los	nos		
l'otra	la otra	**N**	
l'otro	el otro		
luchao	luchado	naa	nada
		nadien	nadie
M		naiden	nadie
		nicles	cinco centavos
		niuno	ni uno
maiz	maíz	no lo	nos lo
malcriao	malcriado	nojaba	enojaba
mandale	mandarle	nojaron	enojaron
mandao	mandado	nojársele	enojársele
manitos	hermanitos	nojón	enojón
manteníanos	manteníamos	nojotras/os	nosotras/os
matalo	matarlo	noo	nuevo
matao	matado	nuevecientos	novecientos
medecina	medicina		
mediano	chico; pequeño	**Ñ**	
menió	meneó		
mentedá	mente	**O**	
mesmas	mismas		
mesmos	mismos	oíanos	oíamos

Glossary

Regional	Standard	Regional	Standard
oiditos	oídos chiquitos	patrás	para atrás
oido	oído	pecao	pecado
ololotes	elotes	pedile	pedirle
olvidao	olvidado	peliao	peliado
onde	donde	pene	un centavo
ónde	dónde	pescalas	pescarlas
ondequiera	dondequiera	pidí	pedí
oportunidá	oportunidad	pidía	pedía
ora	ahora	piensos	pensamientos
orita	ahorita	pior	peor
oyer	oir	pisao	pisado
oyí	oí	plebe	muchachos
		podrían	pudrían

P

Regional	Standard	Regional	Standard
		poo	puedo
		portao	portado
pa	para	pos	pues
pa cas 'e	para casa de	proecito	pobrecito
paá	para allá	precuraba	procuraba
pabajo	para abajo	prencipio	principio
pacá	para acá	puché	empujé
pader	pared	pulla	púa
paí	para allí	pulso	pulsera
pal	para el	pus	pues
pallá	para allá		
panea	pana		
paquel	para aquel		

Q

Regional	Standard	Regional	Standard
parábanos	parábamos	quedábanos	quedábamos
parao	parado	quemalo	quemarlo
paraos	parados	quemao	quemado
parranda	un montón	quemáranos	quemáramos
parriba	para arriba	quisque	quiz que (dicen que)
pasao	pasado		
pasiaban	paseaban	quitábanos	quitábamos
pasiarse	pasearse	quitale	quitarle
pastoriando	pastoreando		

Regional	Standard	Regional	Standard
R		tardecito	un poco tarde
		teneles	tenerlas
Rafel	Rafael	teníanos	teníamos
raiz	raíz	tirale	tirarle
rasguñao	rasguñado	tirao	tirado
rebato	susto	toa	todavía
regüeltas/os	revueltas/os	toas	todas
reinao	reinado	toavía	todavía
rezao	rezado	too	todo
riía	reía	traelas	traerlas
rir	reír	traiba	traía
rirse	reírse	tráibanos	traíamos
rumos	reúma	traido	traído
		trailo	traerlo
S		traque	traqueo; traquido
		traquiaba	traqueteaba
sacale	sacarle	traquió	traqueteó
sacalo	sacarlo	trator	tractor
sacao	sacado	travesiar	travesear
salú	salud	troca	camión;
semejancia	semejanza		camioneta
sentaos	sentados	troviar	trovar
siguía	seguía	trujando	truhaneando
siguimos	seguimos	trujieron	trajeron
silleta/s	silla/s	trujo	trajo
sirvía	servía	tuviéranos	tuviéramos
súbanos	subamos		
subemos	subimos	**U**	
sumetida	sometida		
		usté	usted
T			
		V	
taa	todavía		
taavía	todavía	váyanos	vayamos
tamién	también	velas	verlas

203

Regional	Standard	Regional	Standard
velo	verlo	volao	volado
verdá	verdad	voltiaron	voltearon
vían	veían	voltié	volteé
vide	vi	voltió	volteó
vido	vio	voluntá	voluntad
vinía	venía		
vinir	venir		
visitala	visitarla		
vistían	vestían		
vistida	vestida		
vistirse	vestirse		
vivíanos	vivíamos		
vivo	inteligente	zota	azote; paliza
vo	voy	zoteas	azoteas

W

X

Y

Z

Witchcraft Terms and Expressions Common Among Hispanos of Northern New Mexico

*H*ispanos of Northern New Mexico traditionally have employed a litany of witchcraft terms and expressions as part of their supernatural culture which, to a limited extent, remains alive in many small villages and communities. However, the degree to which these terms are used depends largely on the number of old-timers still living who enjoy and indeed dare to reminisce about witchcraft and its trappings in this technological society we live in today. Some of them savor the thought of telling a good witch story; others are reticent because it is something in their past, seemingly anachronistic and out of touch with modern reality; and finally, there is the customary cynicism even among old-timers themselves who believe that witchcraft was nothing more than a figment of the imagination—although at times, if a *compadre* or a *comadre* fell victim to witchcraft, reality as such seemed more than just a passing fancy.

ambularia (herbolario/a) A woman who specialized in medicinal herbs. Cleofas M. Jaramillo tells us, "Ambularias were graduates in witchcraft and held schools where beginners were taught how to bewitch and how to transform themselves into different things and animals." (*Shadows of the Past/Sombras del Pasado*, Ancient City Press, 1972).

arbolaria, arbularia (herbolario/a) An herbalist who also concocted homemade remedies. Eventually she took it upon herself to eradicate the evildoing of witches. However, at one time an *arbolaria* was thought of as being a witch herself.

¡Ave María Purísima! Holy Mother of God! An expression used when a witch or a ghost appeared in the dead of night. My paternal grandmother employed it to ward off what she perceived to be evil spirits.

bola de cabello A person suspected of having been bewitched often was told by an *arbolaria* or even a *curandero/a* that s/he would discharge a ball of hair as evidence of bewitchment.

bolas de lumbre Fireballs. Reputedly witches in flight, fireballs were mostly seen traversing the skies at night, although some people claim to have seen them during the day.

brasas Literally embers, but in witchcraft jargon people really meant *chispas* (sparks) emitting from a *chiflón* (chimney) of a long-abandoned home suspected of either being inhabited by witches or their spirits.

brujería Sorcery or witchcraft perpetrated by a *bruja* (witch).

brujo/a A witch or sorcerer, usually female, who practiced evil-doings on enemies, or when sought after to inflict harm on someone else because of jealousy or other reasons.

bulto Ghost (not to be confused with a religious statue or *santo*).

cachana A root to ward off evil spirits or witches.

chirrionera (chirronera) Bullwhip snake or simply whip snake. The stories about this snake at one time flourished and varied in scope throughout New Mexico. For example, if an animal or a person stepped on the snake's eggs, the serpent supposedly would whip them (the animal or person) with its tail. Often a man could go bald as a consequence. It should be noted that stories about whip snakes can be found in other parts of the United States.

collar de perlas Bead necklace. This was put on a baby to avoid having it fall victim to the evil eye. At times, as was done in my household, mothers would use a bead bracelet instead, but for the same purpose.

crossed needles People, women especially, who wished to protect their homes from witchlike intrusions would place crossed needles above the doorframe inside the house or on a windowsill. This amounted to, as my paternal grandmother would have said, *ponerle las cruces*, "to make the sign of the cross," in which case a witch was defenseless.

culebra mamoma *Mamona* comes from the verb *mamar*, to suck. This snake was better-known as the milk snake. Many farmers or ranchers believed that if a milk cow had no milk in the morning, a *mamona* had sucked the milk from cow's udder. As a child I heard this story from my paternal grandfather.

curandero/a A folk healer in a community known for curing people with different herbs or remedies from the countryside *(remedios del campo)* or homemade concoctions. Most folk healers did not attempt to treat a patient suspected of suffering from bewitchment. Religion or reliance on faith was and still is an integral part of the folk healer's role in curing a patient.

207

Dios te ponga las cruces "May God Have Pity on You," an expression my paternal grandmother often invoked when something strange appeared (e.g., a ghost or a *bulto*) to ward off the evil being. Similar religious expressions were common in small Hispanic villages to protect them against supernatural creatures at night, which is when they would appear.

duendes These are elves who, according to Aurelio M. Espinosa, represented "evil spirits that terrorize the wicked, lazy, or filthy" ("New Mexican Spanish Folklore," *The Journal of American Folklore*, Vol. XXIII, 1910). Most people I have interviewed knew little if anything about elves or what they signified in terms of the supernatural.

el agüelo The bogeyman (C/f *el coco*).

el basilisco "An ugly bird born from the last egg laid by an old hen," and, "Anyone looked upon by this creature dies instantly,. ..", says Arthur L. Campa (*Hispanic Culture in the Southwest*, University of Oklahoma Press, 1979).

el coco The bogeyman is an ugly, imaginary evil character with supernatural powers, allegedly capable of carrying off naughty children. Expressions such as *si no se callan la boca va venir el coco por ustedes* (if you don't keep quiet the bogey man is going to come after you) were not uncommon in my own household. *El coco* is often used synonymously with the mythical *agüelo*, not to be confused with the real *agüelo* at Christmastime or the one who forms part of the dance group in *Los Matachines*. In both cases his role provides moral underpinnings of sorts for the children.

el diablo The devil. Many stories still abound among old-timers regarding the devil. Narratives vary, but the central focus invariably involves a young, handsome man who appears out of nowhere at a dance and befriends young, beautiful girls. On the spur of the moment one of them would notice strange features, such as hoofs instead of feet, accompanied by a long tail. At that moment the devil would disappear in a puff of sulphurous smoke.

El Libro Negro (Libro de la Magia Negra) *The Black Book* or *Book of Black Magic* contained instruction on how to build or sew objects (e. g., rag dolls, *monos*) with intentions of inflicting harm on a victim.

el mal ojo (el mal de ojo) The evil eye. This, by and large, affects babies or small children when a grownup knowingly—or unknowingly—admires a baby or a child excessively. Fever and incessant crying may follow and, if the baby's illness goes beyond the following Friday, death is imminent. One way to cure the evil eye is for the perpetrator to give the child water from his or her mouth or simply to spit water on the baby's face to "lift" the evil eye.

el tecolote (la lechuza) People believed that a witch had the absolute power to turn into various animals; the owl, also known as a *lechuza*, was a favorite form. Some people thought that a sure way

Witchcraft Terms and Expressions

to kill an owl was to make a cross on the bullet before firing. Often the owl, if injured, turned out to be a local witch or *bruja*.

embrujo Bewitchment. The word comes from *embrujar*, to bewitch. *Embrujo* varied according to the illness inflicted on the victim by the malevolent witch; it could be physical or emotional as well as psychological.

enyerbao (enyerbado) A past participle that comes from the verb *enyerbar*, which literally means to be affected by weeds or herbs which, in most cases, are poisonous. Hence, *enyerbao* signifies to have been poisoned by harmful herbs. In witchcraft, however, as was true in the Río Puerco Valley where I grew up, it meant bewitchment. *Ese hombre está enyerbao*, "that man is bewitched." In some cases a *curandera/o* or an *arbolaria/o* was called for assistance, although in some communities a *médico* or a *médica* was considered more appropriate because they had the knowledge to deal with this type of bewitchment.

espantos Ghosts or ghostlike apparitions. *Espantos* comes from the verb *espantar*, to scare. They tended to appear to anyone at any given time, according to old-timers I have interviewed, but especially to those who went in search of *tesoros enterraos*, buried treasures, thus dissuading them from proceeding with their venture.

guajolote (ajolote) Tadpole or water dog. Young girls were often warned (including in my own family) not to swim in water with tadpoles lest they become pregnant by having these little creatures enter their bodies. This superstition was widespread in New Mexico and is still mentioned by some old-timers today.

hacer ojo To inflict the evil eye (C/f **el mal ojo**).

hechecería The act of witchcraft or sorcery.

hechicero A sorcerer or a witch who inflicts harm on his victims.

Juan/Juana Every village or community had a Juan or Juana who presumably had the power to catch a witch; one favorite way was by turning their clothes wrong-side out. They also possessed the ability to cure a child inflicted with the evil eye.

la cabra The goat. Stories regarding the goat disguised as a witch capable of transporting a person (usually a man with self-serving intentions) at night through the skies from one place to another in short order can still be heard in small Hispanic communities. The Pecos Valley is a case in point.

la cosa mala The evil spirit (literally the evil thing). *La cosa mala*, like all other apparitions or ghosts, customarily appears at night. It can come in the form of a horse, a tattered woman dressed in black, a black dog, and the like.

la lechuza A small owl in New Mexico that often lives inside abandoned prairie-dog mounds. Among Hispanos of Northern New Mexico the *lechuza* and the *tecolote* (C/f *tecolote*) are often one and the same in witchcraft.

La Llorona The Wailing Woman. The stories regarding this popular folkloric figure abound and may well differ from one village to another. One common version is that the Wailing Woman, in a moment of uncontrolled rage, drowned her two children by the river and now roams its banks in search of them. The punishment for her crime is to hear her children's voices every time she walks along the river. *La Llorona* is a universal figure throughout the Spanish-speaking world.

la malora (la mala hora/malogra) The evil hour. The *malora*, as we learn from Aurelio M. Espinosa in the above-mentioned article (C/f **duendes**), "is an evil spirit which wanders about in the darkness of the night at the crossroads and other places. It terrorizes the unfortunate ones who wander alone at night, and has usually the form of a large lock of wool or the whole fleece of wool of a sheep (*un vellón de lana*)."

las ánimas Literally the spirits, although in witchcraft *las ánimas* refers more to those people who are dead and wallowing in purgatory.

las ánimas del purgatorio I learned as a child that *las ánimas* were dead people *(difuntos/dijuntos)* who not only found themselves in purgatory, but who could come and tug at your feet at night while you were asleep if you had been cruel to them while they were on this earth. *Camposantos* (graveyards) supposedly contain many *ánimas en purgatorio*.

la zorra The fox was another favorite animal, in addition to the owl, that witches supposedly liked to turn themselves into.

luces Lights. The stories about fleeting lights, which come in different sizes, are quite prevalent among Hispanic old-timers. To be sure, lights are identified with witches en route to perform some evil scheme.

lugares encantaos Enchanted places. Stories about enchanted places were quite popular among Hispanos. These were sites known for emitting strange sounds or noises at night, sometimes thought of as containing gold or some other buried treasure. In other cases it was thought that the noises simply came from a natural phenomenon of sorts. Regardless, children were admonished never to go near these places possessed by the devil or some other malevolent creature.

maleficiado/a The past participle of *maleficiar,* to cause harm, meaning to be hexed or under the incantation of a witch.

maleficio A spell or bewitchment, *maleficio* applied to any evil or harm administered by a witch.

malhechores Evildoers.

médica A female folk healer. According to Rubén Cobos, a *médica* "invariably combines the function of an *arbolaria*, a *curandera*, a general practitioner, an herbalist, a midwife, and a practical nurse." (*A Dictionary of New Mexico and Southern Colorado Spanish,* Museum of New Mexico Press, 1983).

Witchcraft Terms and Expressions

médico Male folk healer whose specialty, by and large, is herbs. In some communities a *médico* was called upon to perform tasks that dealt with black magic; hence a number of people, such as my maternal grandmother, who was a *curandera,* made the distinction between a *médico* and a *curandera/o.*

mono (monitos) Witches were known to enjoy sticking pins in *monitos,* little rag dolls, often referred to as effigies, as an act of inflicting physical harm on a person. Once the pins were removed, the victim got well.

muñecos Rag dolls or wax figures used by witches to inflict harm.

pactado (pacto) con el diablo It was believed by many people that a witch had a pact with the devil in order to practice evil.

piedra imán Lodestone or magnet which, according to Arthur Campa in *Hispanic Culture in the Southwest,* "was fed steel or iron filings every Friday in order to maintain its strength. The lodestone goes back to Roman times and is an age-old, universal adjunct to the practice of magic."

polvitos Witch powders were capable of casting a spell if a person inadvertently ate some of the witch's food or drank some of her concoctions.

rebato Fright or shock. The word is used synonymously with *susto* in New Mexico.

susto Fright or shock. The word *susto* derives from *asustarse,* to be frightened. *Susto* itself can occur under different circumstances; for example, an encounter with a ghost, a witch, or other supernatural phenomenon such as fireballs. Learning unexpectedly of a relative's tragic death can also cause *susto.* If not treated promptly, it can cause nervous tension, emotional stress, and perhaps even high fever.

tesoros (tesoros enterraos) Buried treasures (C/f *espantos*).

un dijunto (un difunto) A dead person who, in the eyes of some people, often takes on the appearance of an apparition or a ghost whose spirit can come back to haunt a person at night for having crossed it in some way.

visiones Visions or apparitions. Old-timers claim that some individuals had the knack or power to play practical jokes on their own *compadres*, such as having a *cuarta* (quirt) turn into a snake. Men often told stories of having seen ghosts or other *visiones* (strange objects) at night on their way home from a dance. Cynics would accuse them of being drunk, with no truth to their claim.

Witchcraft Terms and Expressions

Creencias/My Childhood Superstitions

As a child I heard, learned, and believed many *creencias* (super-stitions). These beliefs constituted an integral part of my upbringing, although not all of them came from my parents or grandparents. Some I learned from members of my immediate and extended families, while others came from old-timers in my community of Guadalupe (Ojo del Padre) in the Río Puerco valley. As a boy I believed many of them, especially those that my parents used that made me and my brothers panic, such as, "Don't play with fire before bedtime or you'll wet the bed".

As I grew older, I became quite suspicious of many of the super-stitions I had been exposed to, so I began to reject some of them. Others, however, still form part of my persona. For example, as a small boy I never left hairs in the wash basin, fearful that they would indeed turn to snakes. Today I no longer believe in that supersti-tion, but I do maintain the ritual more as a matter of habit than anything else.

The following superstitions are those that I grew up with on the farm and that I can still recall. Others no doubt have gone by the wayside.

- ❧ *No dejes cabellos en la bandeja o se vuelven víboras*
  Don't leave hair in the washbasin or they'll turn into snakes

- ❧ *No juegues con sapos o te salen mezquinos (por ej., en las manos)*
  Don't play with frogs or you'll get warts (e.g., on your hands)

- ❧ *Pa quitarte los mezquinos, cuéntalos y pon el mesmo número de piedritas en un saquito de tabaco y tíralo—a alguien le va tocar los mezquinos*
  To get rid of warts, count them and put an equal number of pebbles in a small sack (tobacco-size) and dispose of it—some-one else will get them

- ❧ *Si jallas fruta alderedor de la casa, no te la comas (especialmente si no hay güerta o árboles de fruta); alguien te quiere hacer mal*

Don't eat fruit found around the house (especially if there are no orchards or fruit trees); somebody may be trying to bewitch you

❧ *No juegues con lumbre o fósforos antes de acostarte o te vas a mear en la cama*
Don't play with fire or matches before bedtime or you'll wet the bed

❧ *Si hablas de alguien que está muerto, di "Que descanse en paz," o te puede venir a jalar los pies en la cama*
When speaking of someone who is dead, say, "May s/he rest in peace," lest that person come and pull at your feet while you're in bed

❧ *Haz la señal de la cruz cuando pases por la iglesia o te toca mala suerte*
Be sure to make the sign of the cross when going past a church or bad luck will come to you

❧ *Quítate (remúdate) el sombrero cuando pases por la iglesia o Dios te castiga*
Be sure to take off your hat when passing by (in front of) a church or God will punish you

❧ *Si se mete un pajarito en tu casa, alguien va murir*
If a bird flies into your home, someone is going to die

215

❧ *Si una persona mira una criatura (un niño) muncho, le puede hacer (mal) ojo*
If a person admires a baby too much, it can become the victim of the evil eye

❧ *Si estrellas un espejo, te tocan varios años de mala suerte*
If you break a mirror, you'll be faced with several years of bad luck

❧ *Nunca mires la hostia en la misa o te castiga Dios*
Never look at the host in church or God is going to punish you

❧ *Le pegas a tu padre y se te va secar el brazo (la mano)*
Strike your father and your arm's going to shrivel up
or
Strike your father and the ground will swallow you up to the waistline and you'll roam the four corners of the earth for the rest of your life

❧ *Si desea algo que alguien está comiendo, te va salir un granito en la*

Creencias/My Childhood Superstitions

punta de la lengua
If you see someone eating something (e.g., dessert) you wish you could have, but can't, you'll develop a sore at the tip of your tongue

⚕ *Si miras un perro meándose, te va salir un chilito de perro*
Should you see a dog peeing, you're going to get a sty in one eye shut.

⚕ *Si duermes con la ventana abierta, vas amanecer con un ojo gacho*
If you sleep next to an open window, you'll wake up with one eye shut

⚕ *Lávate la cara todas las mañanas con agua fría y no te salen arrugas*
Wash your face every morning with cold water and you won't get wrinkles

⚕ *Lávate la cara con agua fría cada mañana y vives más tiempo*
Wash your face with cold water every morning and you'll live longer

⚕ *Si te sale un bulto, ponle las cruces y se desparece*
If a ghost appears before you (at night), make a cross using your thumb and index finger (right hand), utter the words, *Póngate las cruces*, and it will disappear

⚕ *Si se te cae una cuchara en el suelo, alguien viene a verte*
If you drop a spoon on the floor, someone's coming to visit you

⚕ *Si rezas que caiga agua, pero no cae, castígate a los santos y llueve*
If you pray for rain, but none comes, punish the *santos* (saints) (e.g., make them face the wall) and they'll respond

⚕ *Si el cielo está emborregado, es que va cae muncha agua*
If the sky is full of sheeplike clouds, it's because it's going to rain a lot

⚕ *Cuando están las nubes colora(d)as, es porque va ser viento*
When the clouds are rosy red, it's because it's going to be windy

⚕ *Salen sapos (ranas) en las lagunas después de unas güenas lluvias*
Frogs will appear in lagoons after heavy rains or thunderstorms

⚕ *Si se cae una estrella del cielo y va dar al suelo, se acaba el mundo*
A falling star will destroy the earth if it hits the ground

Creencias/My Childhood Superstitions

☞ *Si se está lavando la cara el gato, es porque viene gente*
If a cat washes its face, people are coming to visit

☞ *Mójate la mollera en el verano o te vas asolear (asollamar)*
Wet the top of your head on a hot summer day before swimming or you'll get a sunstroke

☞ *Si te sale sangre de la nariz, ponte un centavo en la frente pa que se te quite*
Whenever you have a nose bleed, put a coin (a penny) on your forehead to make it stop

☞ *Si canta un gallo en el día, el tiempo se va descomponer*
If a rooster crows during the day, the weather's bound to turn nasty

☞ *No le hagas cosquillas al niño en la planta de los pies o se le acaba el resuello*
Don't tickle the baby on the bottom of his feet or he'll lose his breath

☞ *No le cortes las uñas al niño si no le cortas la fuerza del cuerpo*
Don't cut the baby's fingernails or else you'll cut off its circulation

217

☞ *Si quieres que se te quiten los rumos, ponte un pulso de cobre en la muñeca*
If you want your rheumatism to go away, put on a copper bracelet

☞ *Si te cortas un dedo, ponte un cuchillo frío en la rajada pa que no te sangres*
If you cut your finger, put a cold knife (the blade) on the cut to stop the bleeding

☞ *Si quieres pescar las brujas, voltéate la camiseta al revés*
If you wish to catch the witches, turn your t-shirt inside out

☞ *No comas carne de marrano pa le cena o vas oyer los marranos en la cama toa la noche*
Don't eat pork for supper or you'll hear pig's noise in bed all night long

Creencias/My Childhood Superstitions

Villanueva—Arts and Crafts

Suggested Reading

Anaya, Rudolfo A., and José Griego y Maestas. *Cuentos: Tales from the Hispanic Southwest*. Santa Fe: Museum of New Mexico Press, 1980.

——. *The Legend of La Llorona*. A short novel. Berkeley: Tonatiuh-Quinto Sol International, Inc., 1984.

Aragón, Ray John de. *The Legend of La Llorona*. Las Vegas, NM: The Pan American Publishing CO., 1980.

Benavides Sumpter, Magdalena, ed. *Discovering Folklore Through Community Resources*. Austin, TX: Migrant Inservice and Curriculum Development, P.S.J.A. School District, 1978.

Espinosa, Aurelio M., ed. J. Manuel Espinosa. *The Folklore of Spain in the American Southwest*. Norman: University of Oklahoma Press, 1985.

——. *Cuentos populares españoles*. Tomo I. Stanford University Publications, 1923; reprint, New York: AMS Press, Inc., 1967.

Espinosa, José Manuel. *Spanish Folk-Tales from New Mexico*. New York: The American Folk-Lore Society, 1937; reprint, New York: Kraus Reprint Co., 1976

García, Nasario. *Recuerdos de los viejitos: Tales of the Río Puerco*. Albuquerque: University of New Mexico Press, 1987.

——. *Abuelitos: Stories of the Río Puerco Valley*. Albuquerque: University of New Mexico Press, 1992.

——. *Comadres: Hispanic Women of the Río Puerco Valley*. Albuquerque: University of New Mexico Press 1997.

——. *Más antes: Hispanic Folklore of the Río Puerco Valley*. Museum of New Mexico Press, 1997.

Jameson, R.D., ed. Stanley L. Robe. *Hispanic Folktales from New Mexico*. Los Angeles: University of California Press, 1977.

——. ed. Standley L. Robe. *Hispanic Legends from New Mexico*. Los Angeles: University of California Press, 1980.

219

Jaramillo, Cleofas M. *Shadows of the Past/Sombras del pasado*. Santa Fe: Seton Village, 1941; reprint, Santa Fe: Ancient City Press, 1972.

Rael, Juan B. *Cuentos españoles de Colorado y Nuevo México (Spanish Folk Tales from Colorado and New Mexico)*. 2d ed. revised, Vols. I & II. Santa Fe: Museum of New Mexico Press, 1977; 1st ed., Stanford University Press, date unknown.

Simmons, Marc. *Witchcraft in the Southwest: Spanish and Indian Supernaturalism on the Río Grande*. Flagstaff, AZ: Northland Press, 1974.

Weigle, Marta, and Peter White. *The Lore of New Mexico*. Albuquerque: University of New Mexico Press, 1988.

West, John O. *Mexican-American Folklore*. Little Rock: August House Publishers, 1988.

Suggested Reading